Theodore Gericault:
101 Paintings and Drawings

By Maria Tsaneva

First Edition

*****

Foreword

Jean-Louis André Théodore Géricault (1791 – 1824) was an influential French painter and lithographer, known for The Raft of the Medusa and other paintings. Although he died young, he was one of the pioneers of the Romantic Movement. His stormy career lasted little more than a decade and in that time he displayed a meteoric and many-sided genius. His love of thrilling action, his sense of swirling movement, his energetic conduct of paint, and his taste for the horrid were all to become features of Romanticism. Géricault was, at the same time avant-garde in his realism: he made studies from corpses and severed limbs for The Raft of the Medusa and painted an extraordinary series of portraits of mental patients in the clinic of his friend Dr Georget. His work had enormous influence, most notably on Delacroix.

Born in Rouen, France, Géricault was educated in the tradition of English sporting art by Carle Vernet and classical figure composition by Pierre-Narcisse Guérin, a rigorous classicist who disapproved of his student's impulsive temperament yet recognized his talent. Géricault soon left the classroom, choosing to study at the Louvre, where from 1810 to 1815 he copied paintings by Rubens, Titian, Velázquez and Rembrandt. During this period at the Louvre he discovered a vitality he found lacking in the prevailing school of Neoclassicism. Much of his time was spent in Versailles, where he found the stables of the palace open to him, and where he gained his knowledge of the anatomy and action of horses.

Géricault's first major work, The Charging Chasseur, exhibited at the Paris Salon of 1812, revealed the influence of the style of Rubens and an interest in the depiction of contemporary subject matter.

This youthful success, ambitious and monumental, was followed by a change in direction: for the next several years Géricault produced a series of small studies of horses and cavalrymen. He exhibited Wounded Cuirassier at the Salon in 1814, a work more labored and less well received. Géricault in a fit of disappointment entered the army and served for a time in the garrison of Versailles. In the nearly two years that followed the 1814 Salon, he also underwent a self-imposed study of figure construction and composition, all the while evidencing a personal predilection for drama and expressive force.

A trip to Florence, Rome, and Naples (1816–17), prompted in part by the desire to flee from a romantic entanglement with his aunt, ignited a fascination with Michelangelo. Rome itself inspired the preparation of a monumental canvas, the Race of the Barberi Horses, a work of epic composition and abstracted theme that promised to be "entirely without parallel in its time". In the event, Géricault never completed the painting, and returned to France. In 1821, he painted The Derby of Epsom.

Géricault continually returned to the military themes of his early paintings, and the series of lithographs he undertook on military subjects after his return from Italy are considered some of the earliest masterworks in that medium. Perhaps his most significant, and certainly most ambitious work, is The Raft of the Medusa (1818–1819), which depicted the aftermath of a contemporary French shipwreck, Meduse, in which the captain had left the crew and passengers to die. The incident became a national scandal, and Géricault's dramatic interpretation presented a contemporary tragedy on a monumental scale. The painting's notoriety stemmed from its indictment of a corrupt establishment, but it also dramatized a more eternal theme, that of man's struggle with nature. It surely excited the imagination of the young Eugène Delacroix, who posed for one of the dying figures.

The classical depiction of the figures and structure of the composition stand in contrast to the turbulence of the subject, so that the painting constitutes an important bridge between neo-classicism and romanticism. It fuses many influences: the Last Judgment of Michelangelo, the monumental approach to contemporary events by Antoine-Jean Gros, figure groupings by Henry Fuseli, and possibly the painting Watson and the Shark by John Singleton Copley.

The painting ignited political controversy when first exhibited at the Paris Salon of 1819; it then traveled to England in 1820, accompanied by Géricault himself, where it received much praise. While in London, Géricault witnessed urban poverty, made drawings of his impressions, and published lithographs based on these observations which were free of sentimentality. He associated much there with Charlet, the lithographer and caricaturist.

After his return to France in 1821, Géricault was inspired to paint a series of ten portraits of the insane, the patients of a friend, Dr. Étienne-Jean Georget, a pioneer in psychiatric medicine, with each subject exhibiting a different affliction. There are five remaining portraits from the series, including Insane Woman. The paintings are noteworthy for their bravura style, expressive realism, and for their documenting of the psychological discomfort of individuals, made all the more poignant by the history of insanity in Géricault's family, as well as the artist's own fragile mental health. His observations of the human subject were not confined to the living, for some remarkable still-lifes — painted studies of severed heads and limbs — have also been ascribed to the artist. Géricault's last efforts were directed toward preliminary studies for several epic compositions, including the Opening of the Doors of the Spanish Inquisition and the African Slave Trade. The preparatory drawings suggest works of great ambition, but Géricault's waning health intervened.

Weakened by riding accidents and chronic tubercular infection, Géricault died in Paris in 1824 after a long period of suffering. His bronze figure reclines, brush in hand, on his tomb at Père Lachaise Cemetery in Paris, above a low-relief panel of The Raft of the Medusa.

Paintings and Drawings

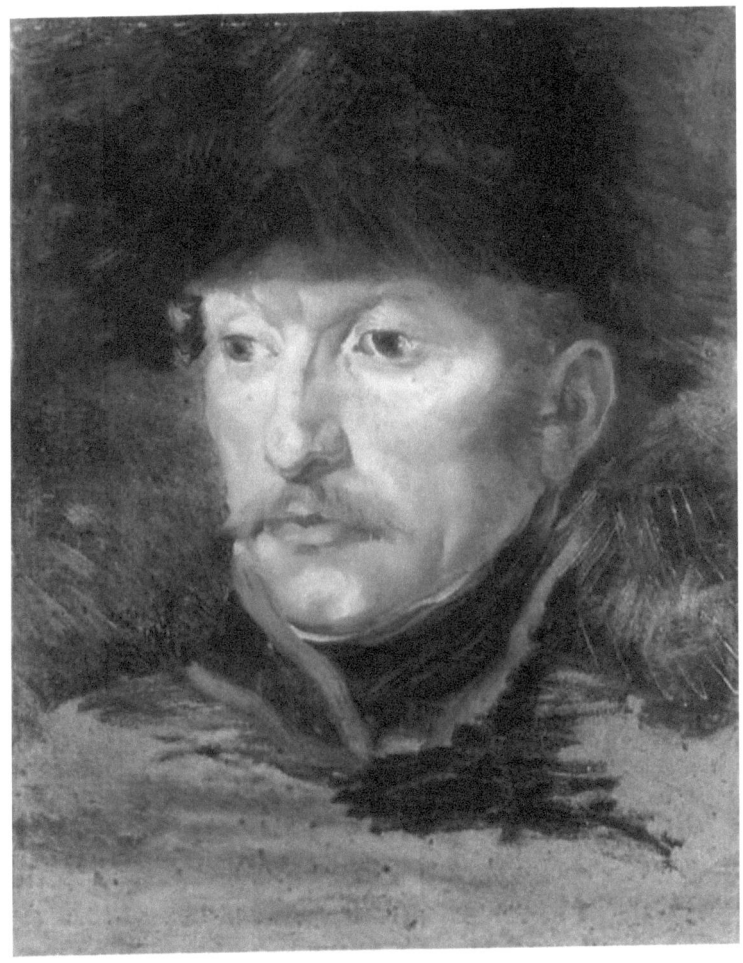

Head of a horseman, c.1812
Oil on canvas

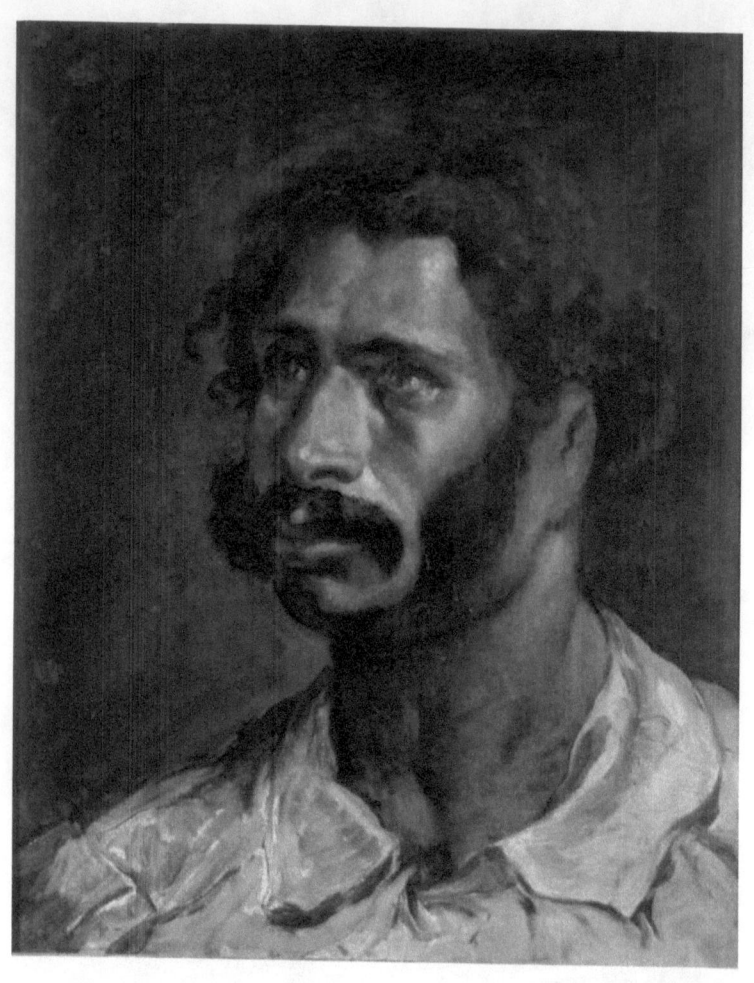

Portrait of the Carpenter of The Medusa, c.1812
Oil on canvas

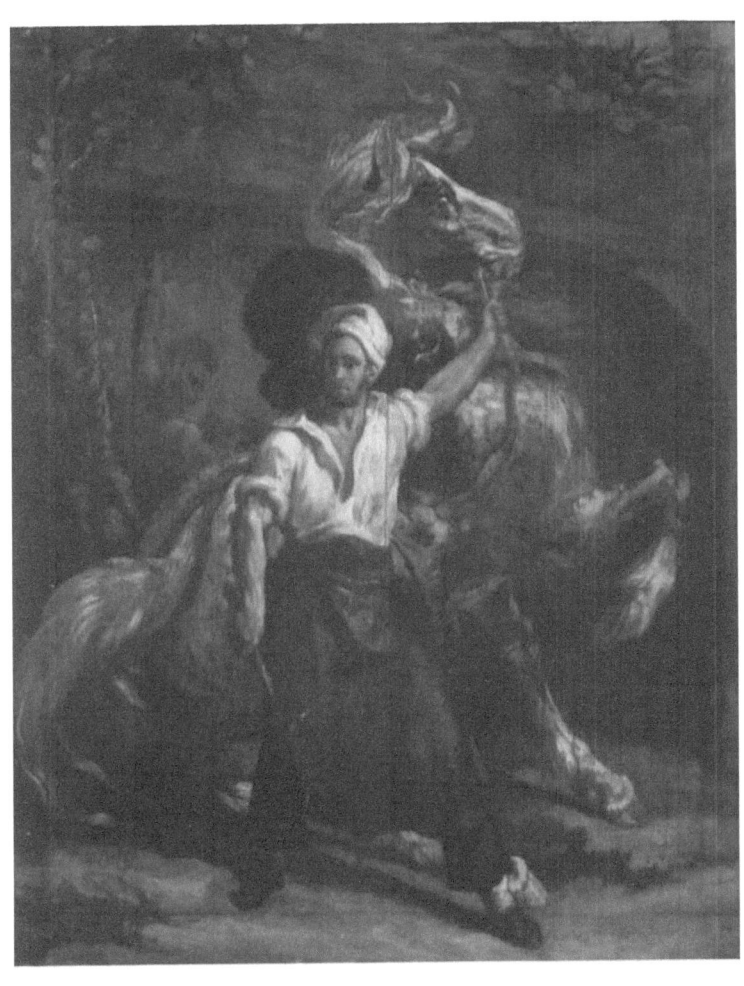

The Blacksmith's Signboard, 1814
Oil on canvas

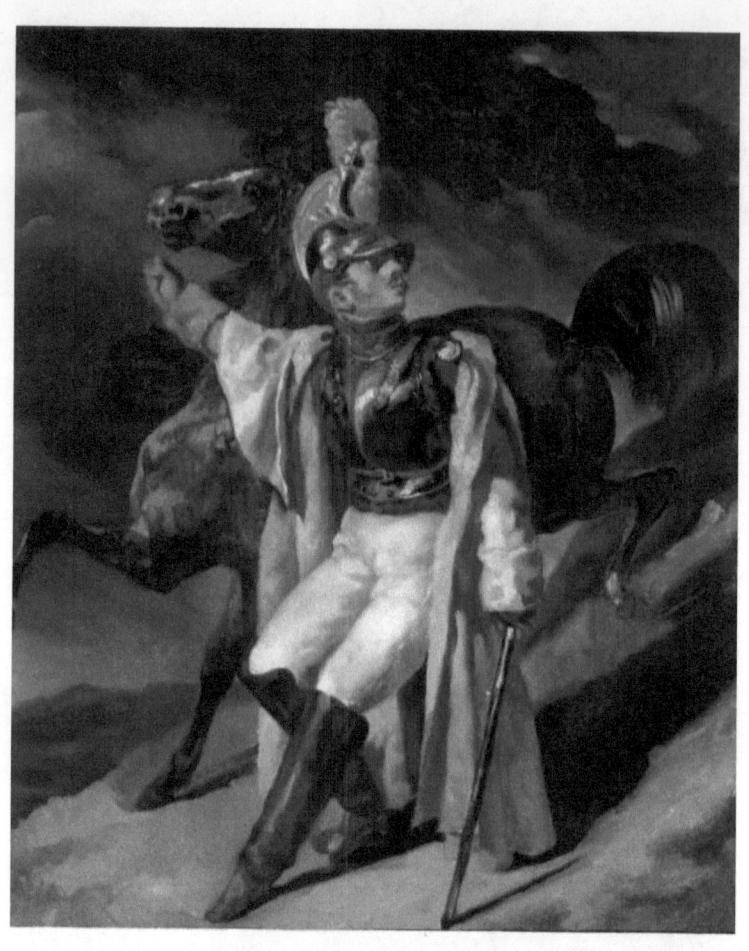

The Wounded Cuirassier, 1814
Oil on canvas

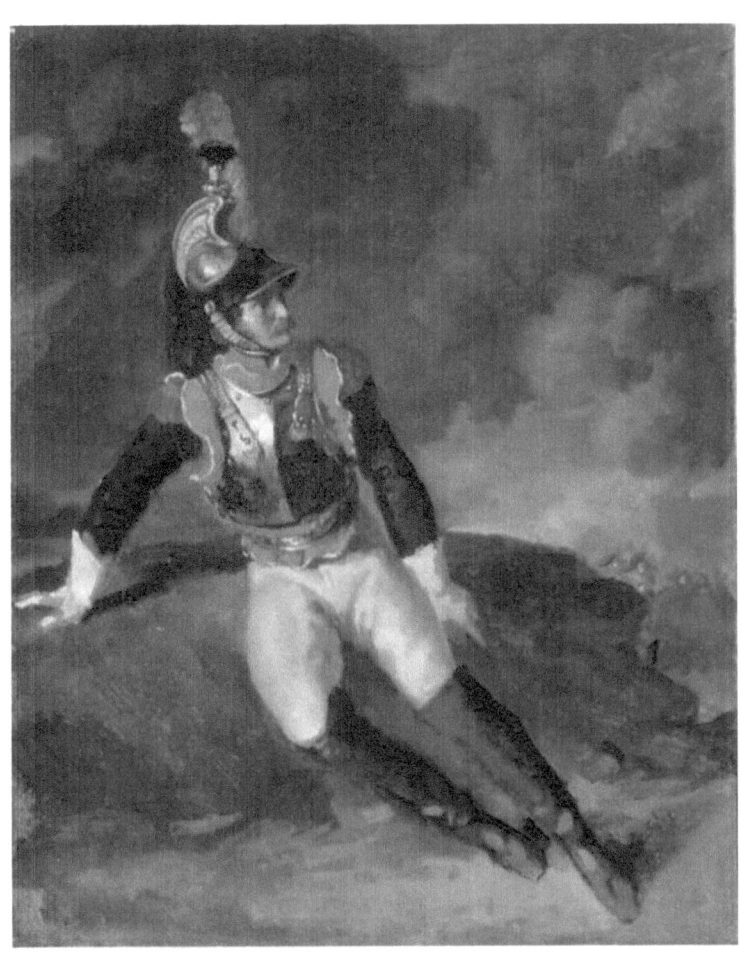

The Wounded Cuirassier, 1814
Oil on canvas

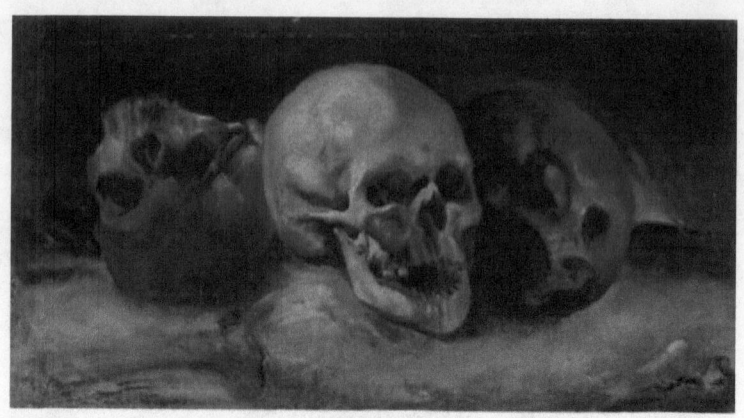

The three skulls, 1812-1814
Oil on canvas

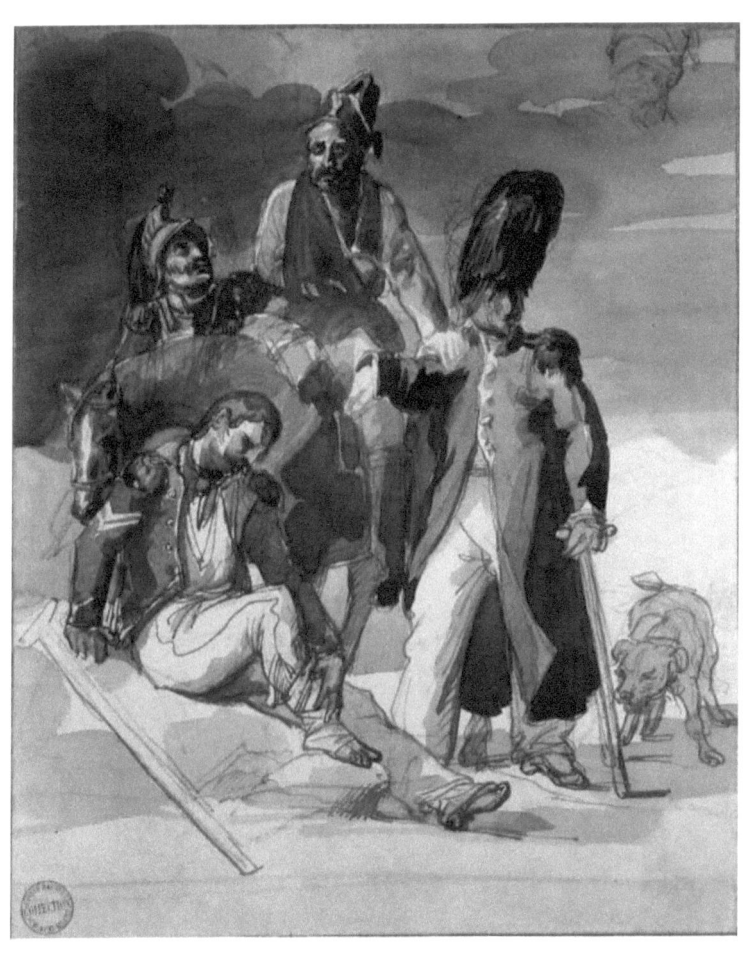

Wounded Soldiers Retrating from Russia, c. 1814
Pencil, pen and brown ink, watercolour

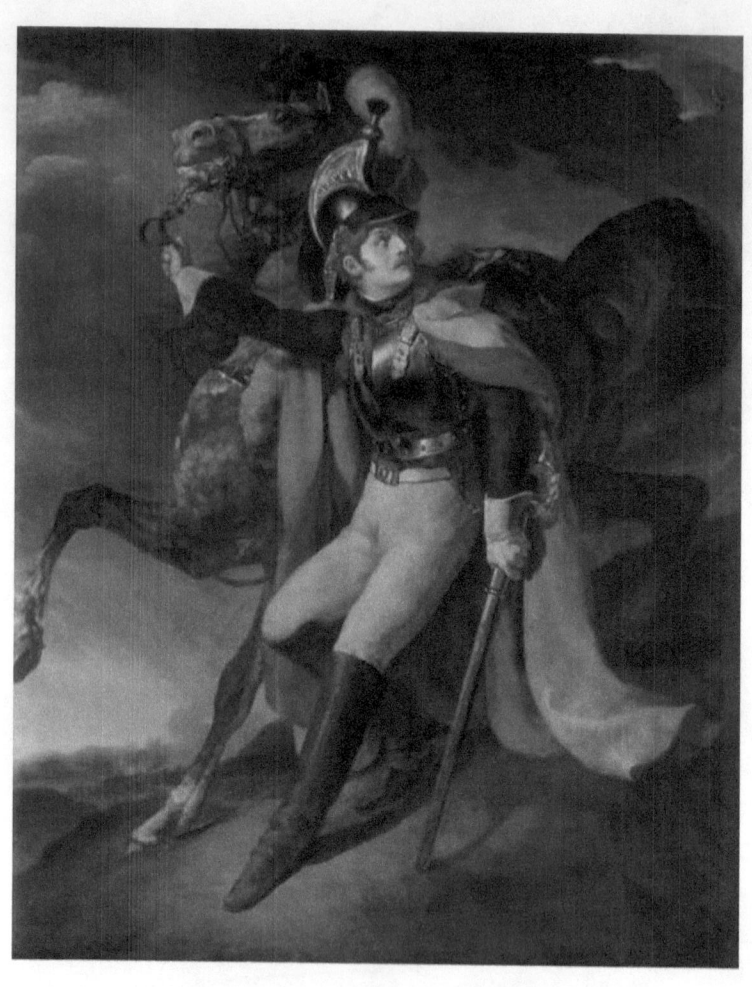

Wounded Cuirassier, 1814
Oil on canvas

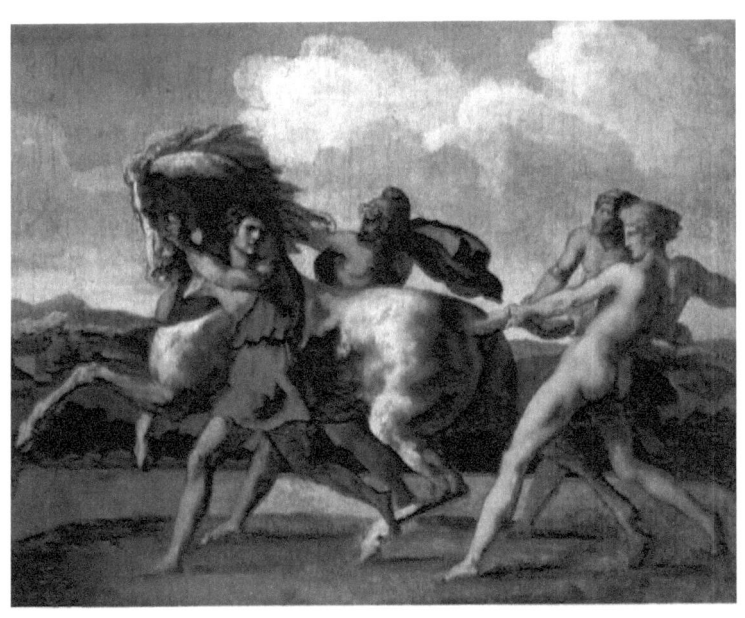

Slaves stopping a horse, study for The Race of the
Barbarian Horses, 1817
Oil on canvas

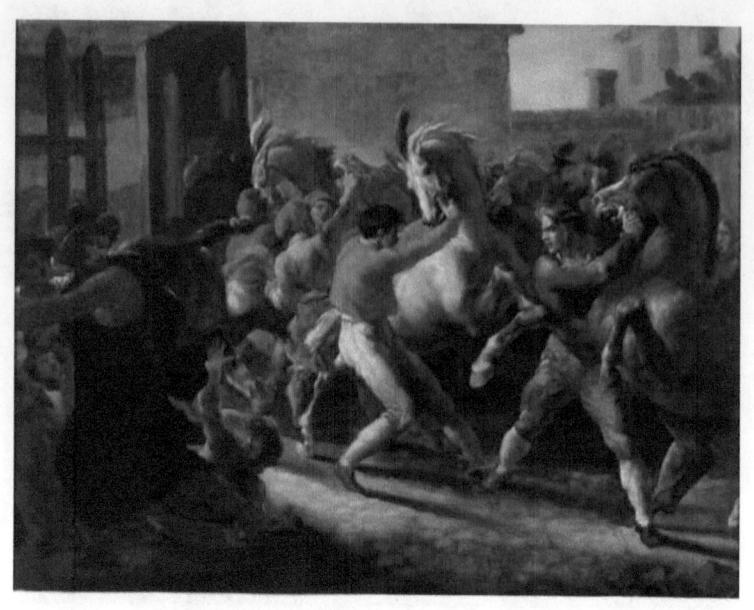

Study for the Race of the Barbarian Horses, 1817
Oil on canvas

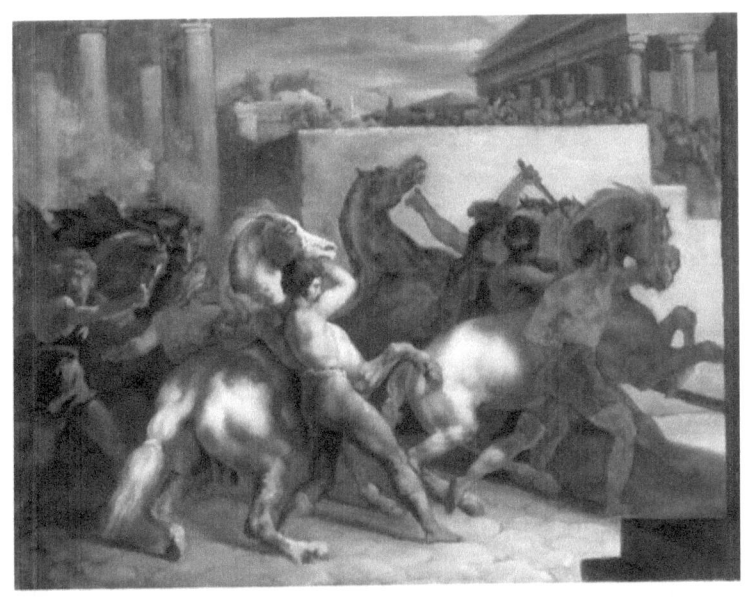

The Wild Horse Race at Rome, 1817
Oil on canvas

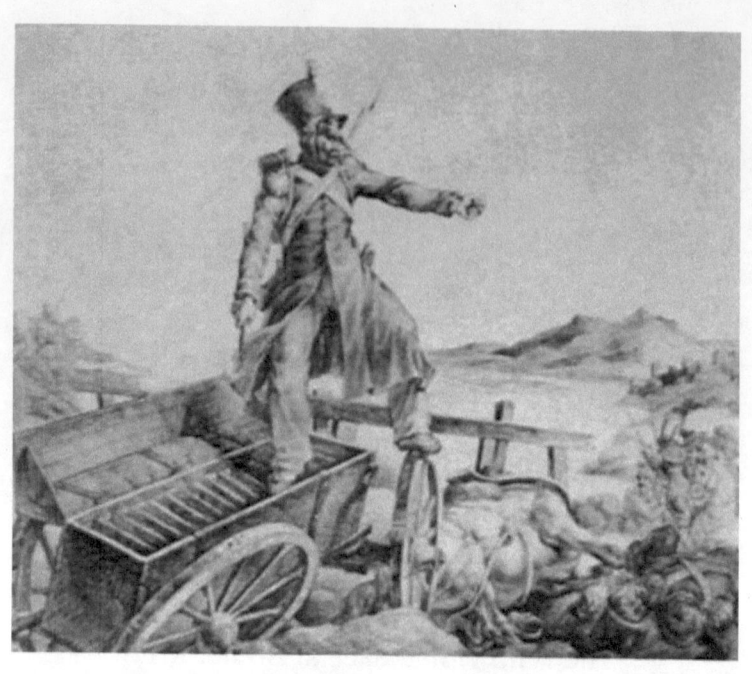

Artillery caisson, 1818
Drawing

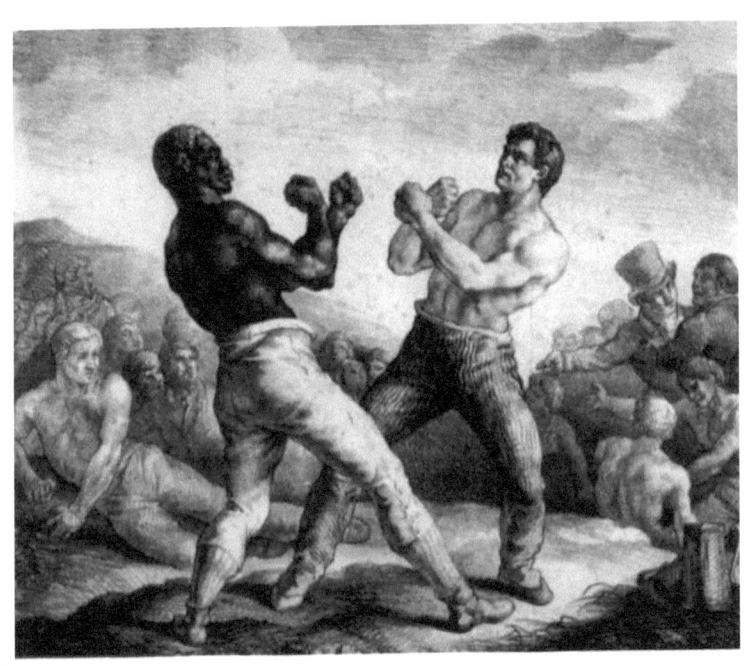

Boxers, 1818
Drawing

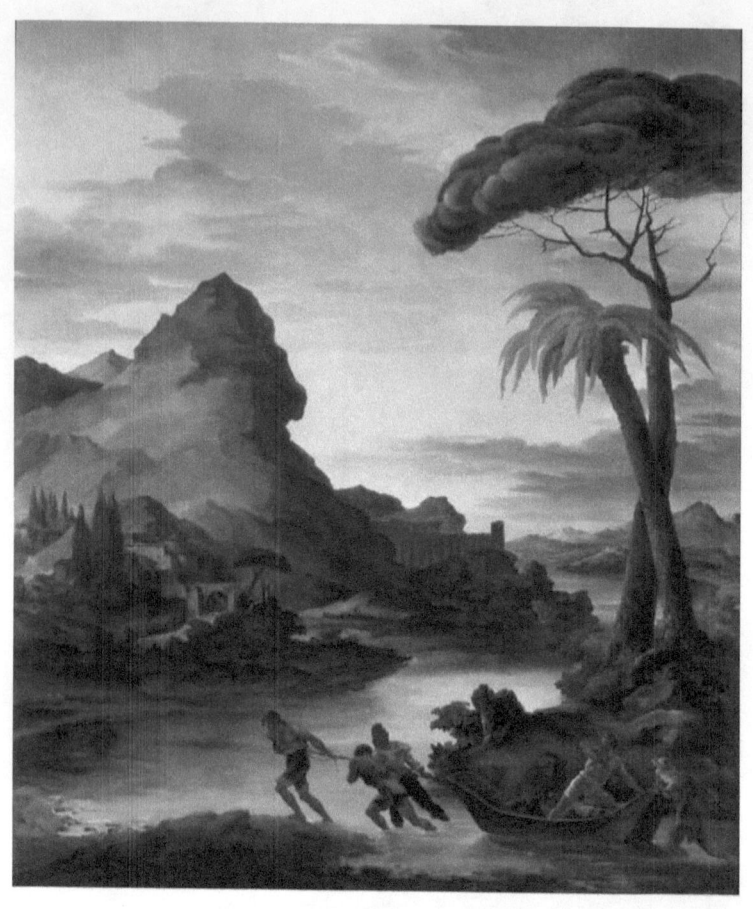

Heroic Landscape with Fishermen, 1818
Oil on canvas

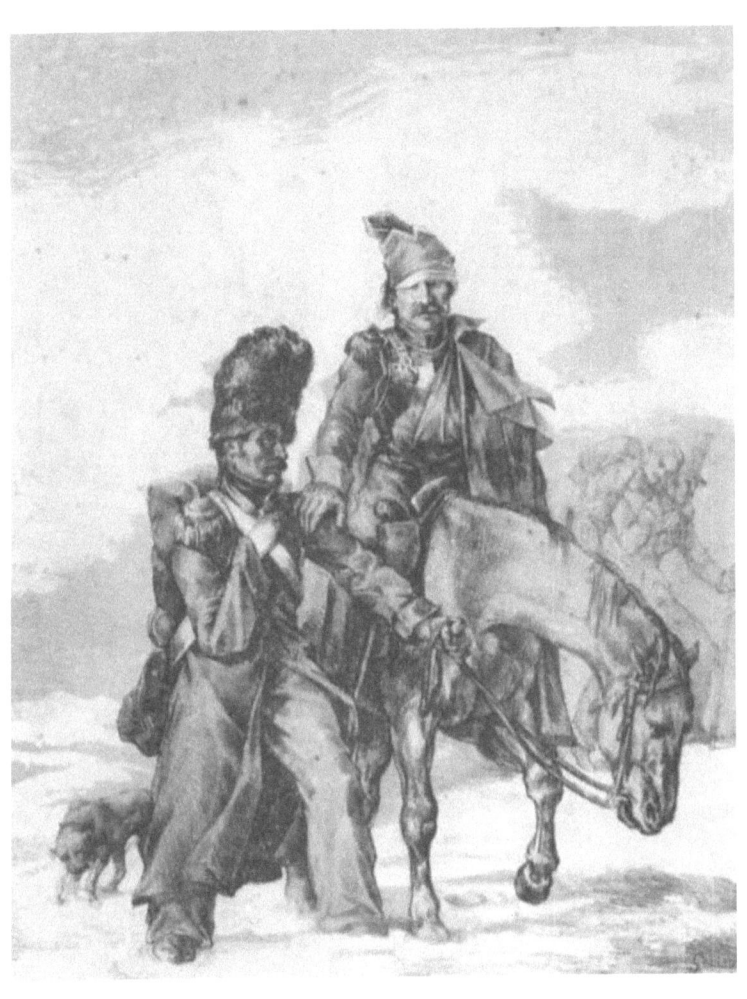

The Return from Russia, 1818
Drawing

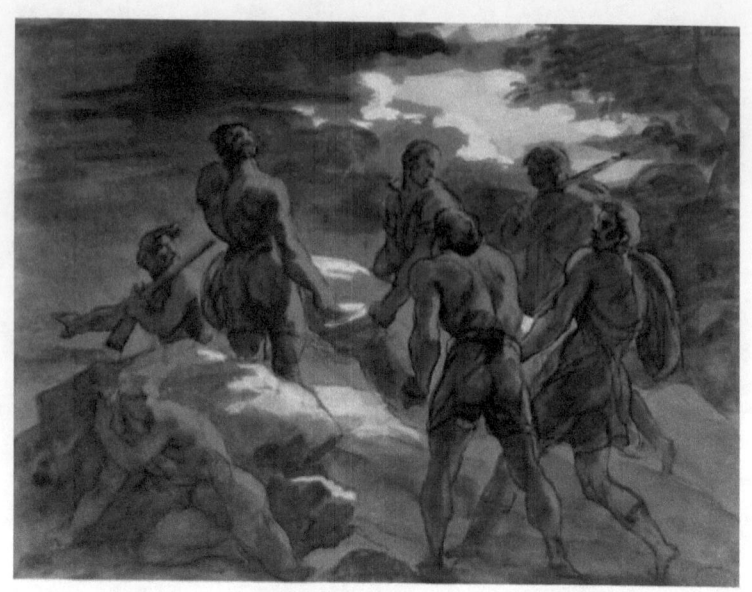

The murderers carry the body of Fualdes, 1818
Drawing

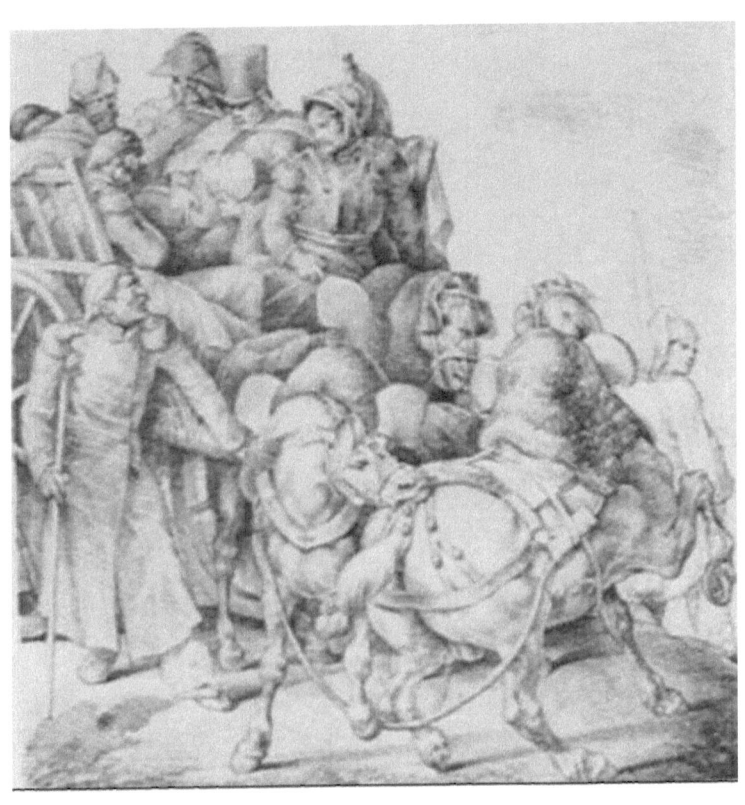

Wagons filled with wounded soldiers, 1818

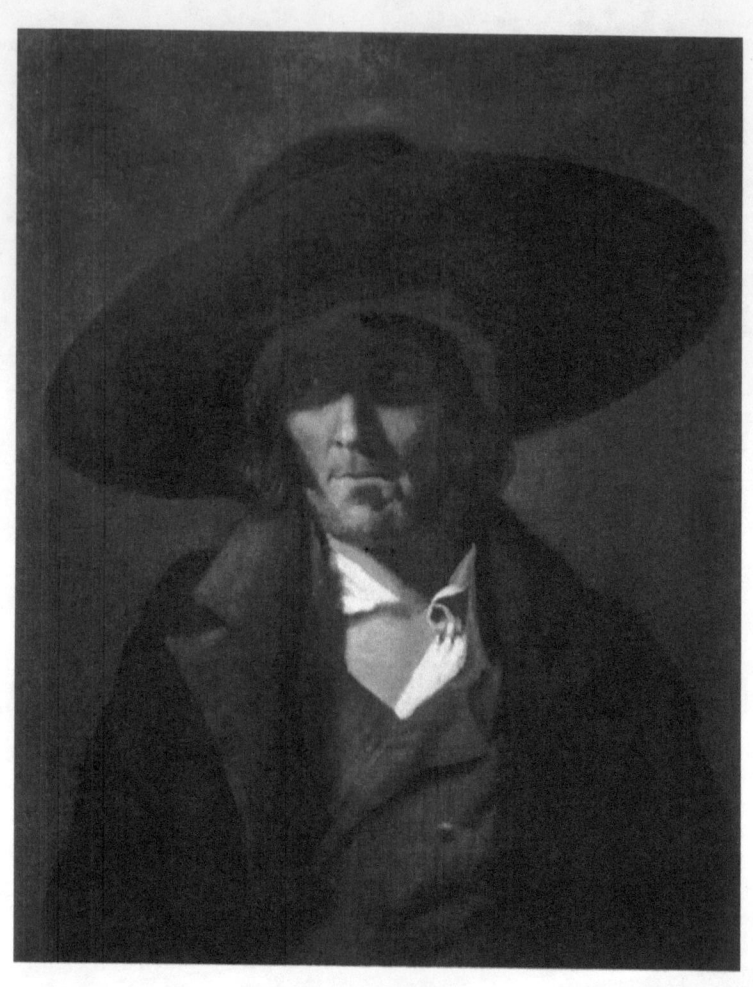

A man, 1815-1819
Oil on canvas

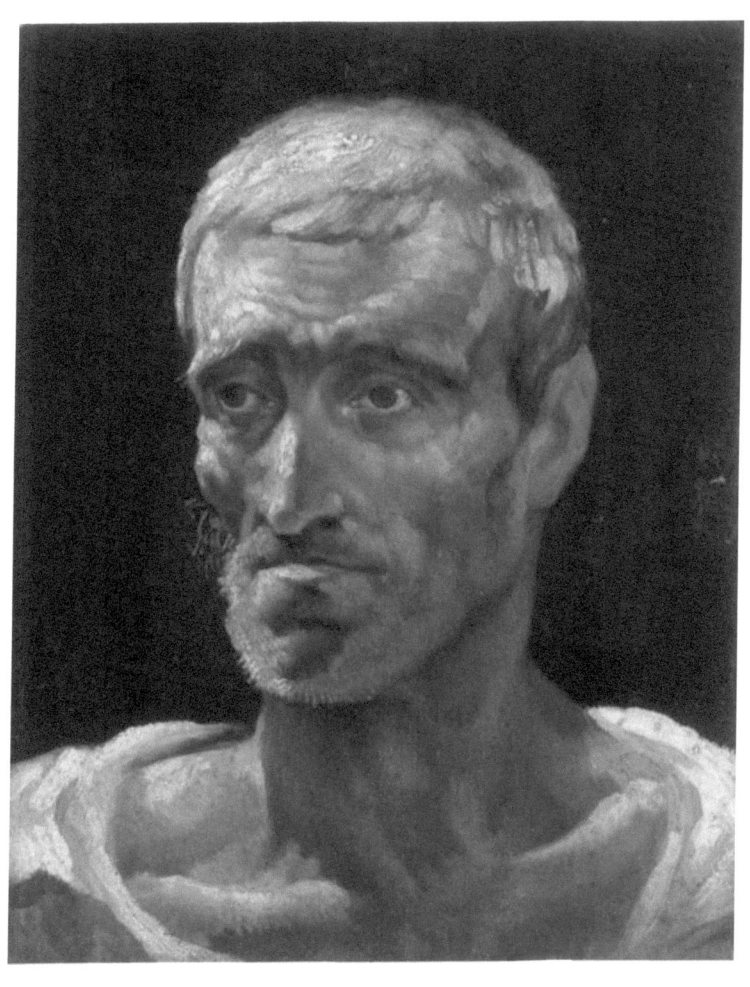

Head of a Shipwrecked Man (study for the Raft of
Medusa), 1817-1819
Oil on canvas

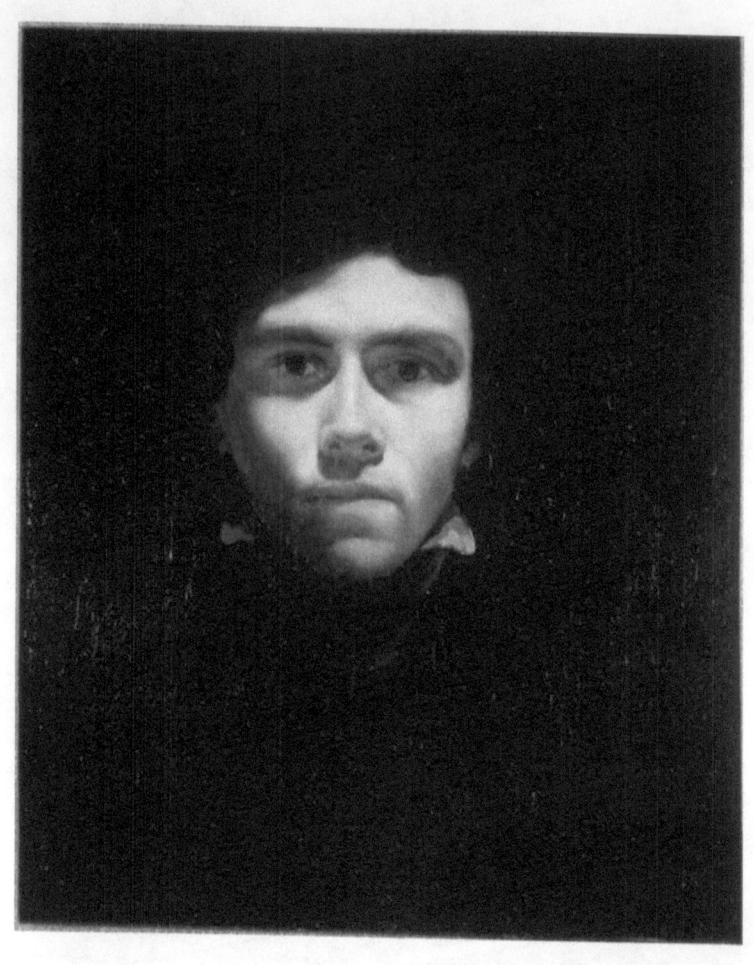

Portrait of Eugene Delacroix, 1818-1819
Oil on canvas

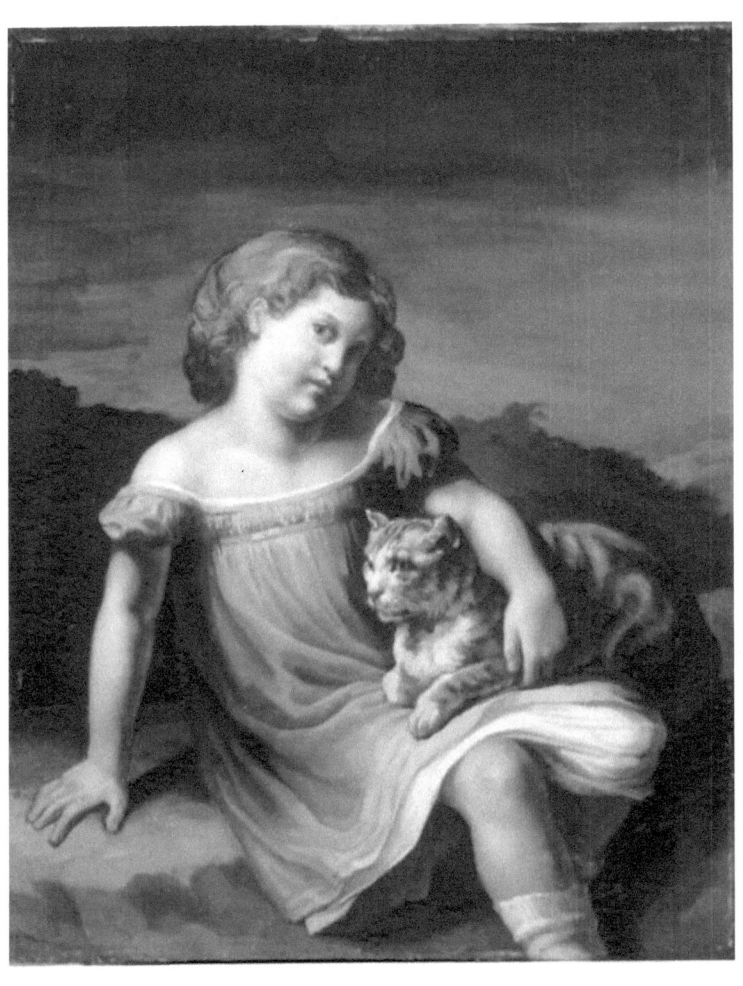

Portrait of Louise Vernet as a Child, 1818-1819
Oil on canvas

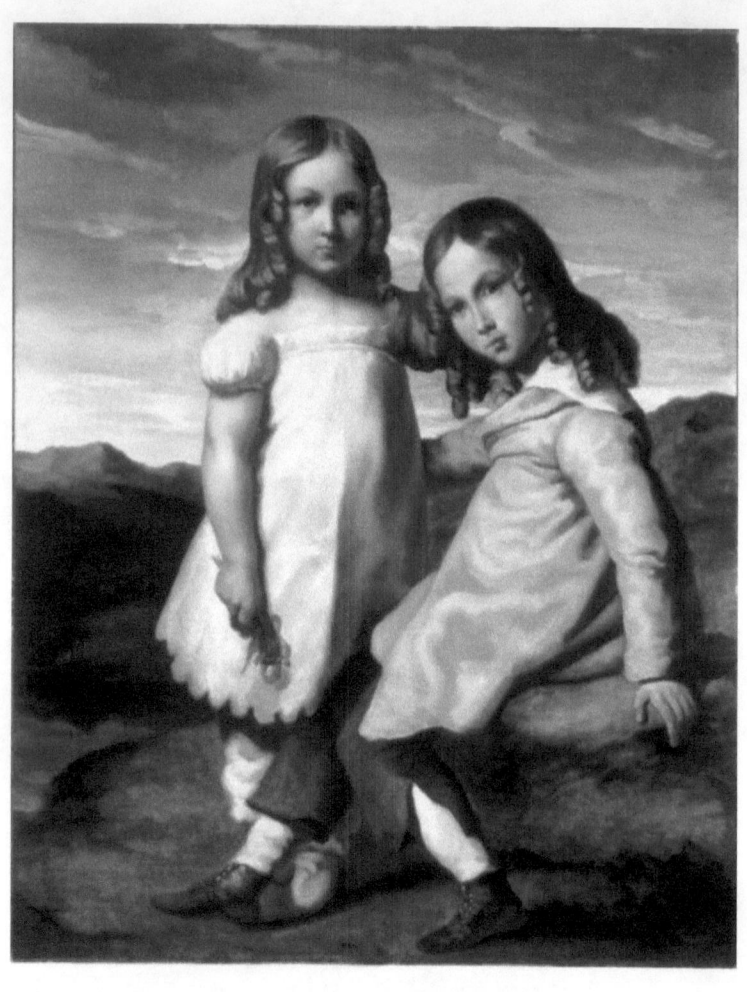

Portrait of Alfred and Elizabeth Dedreux, 1817-1819
Oil on canvas

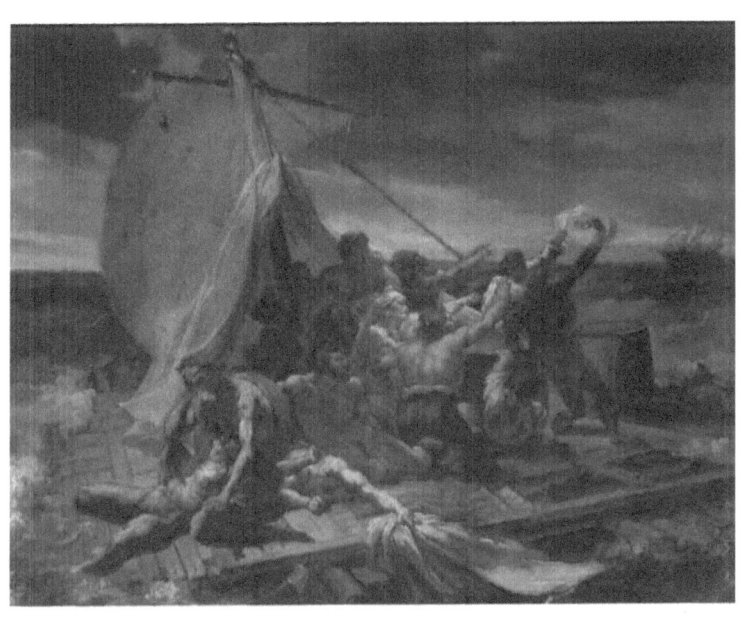

Study for The Raft of the Medusa, 1819
Oil on canvas

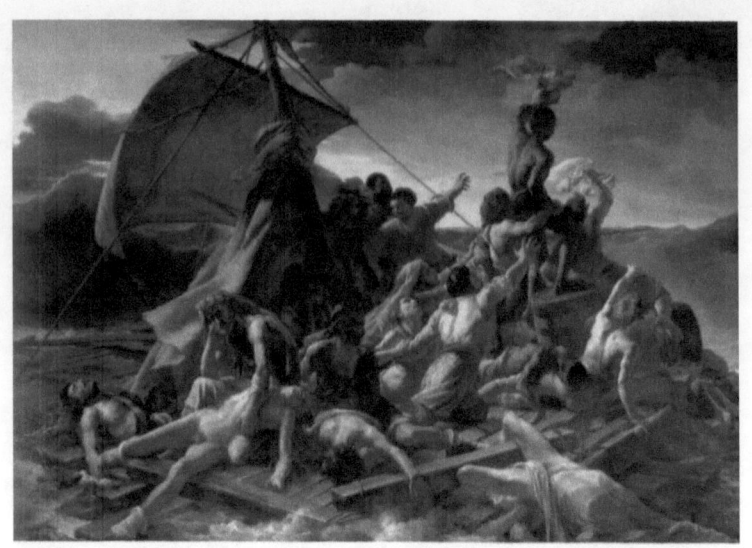

The Raft of the Medusa, 1818-1819
Oil on canvas

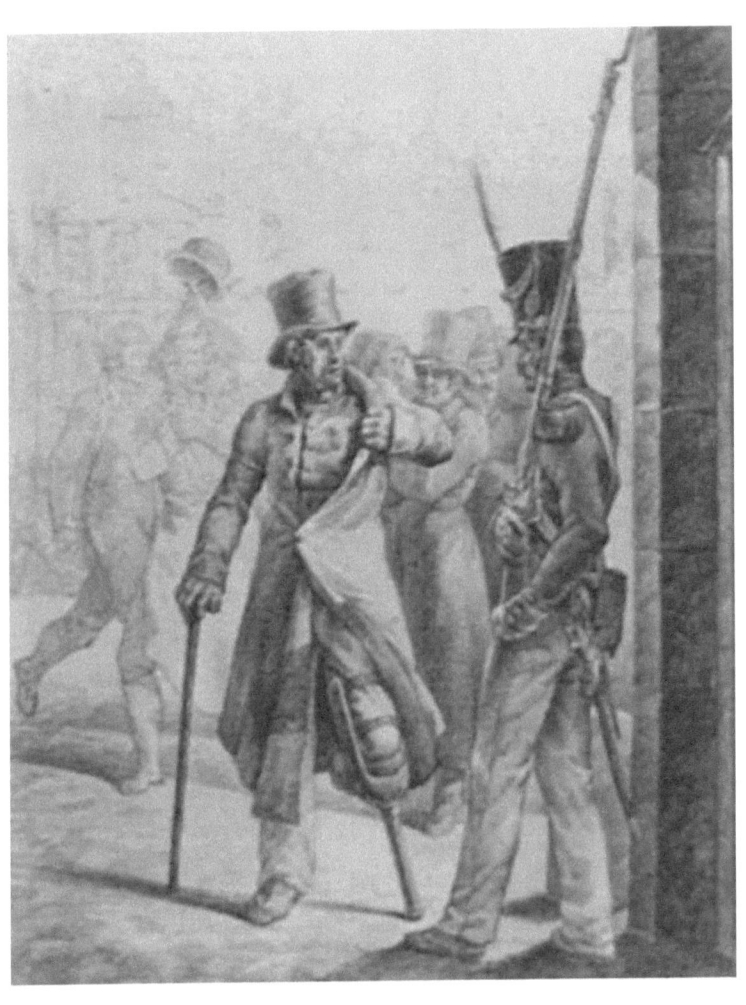

The Swiss guard at the Louvre, 1819
Drawing

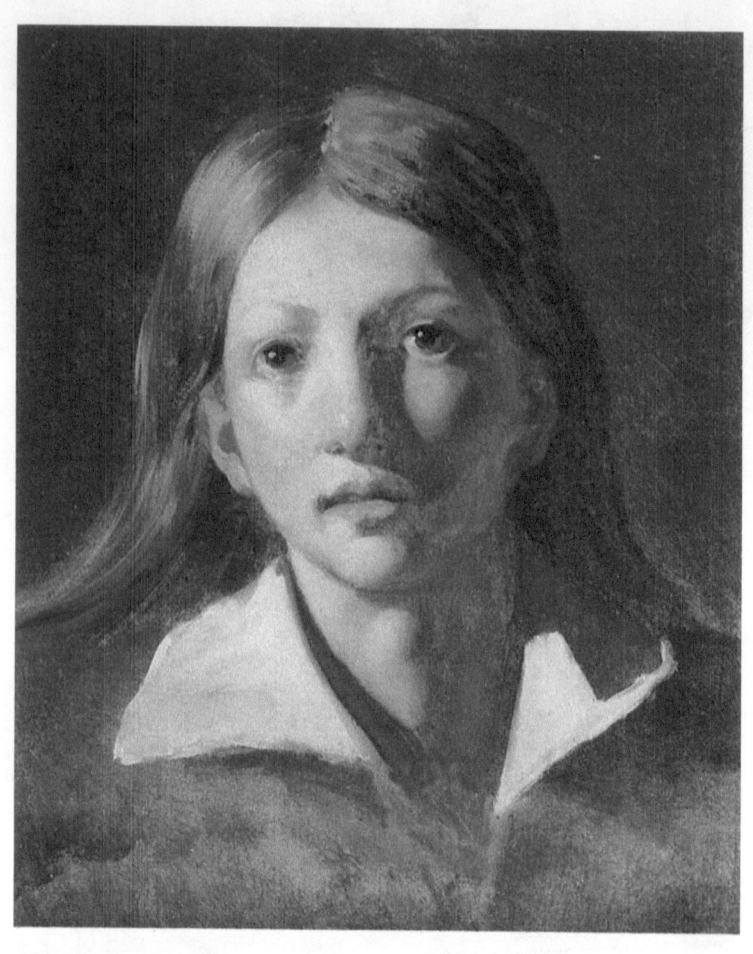

Young blond man, 1818-1819
Oil on canvas

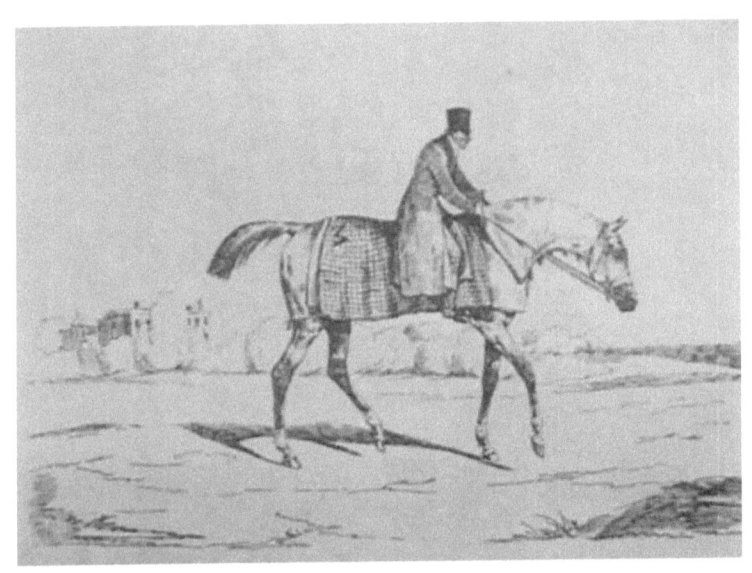

English Jockey, 1820
Drawing

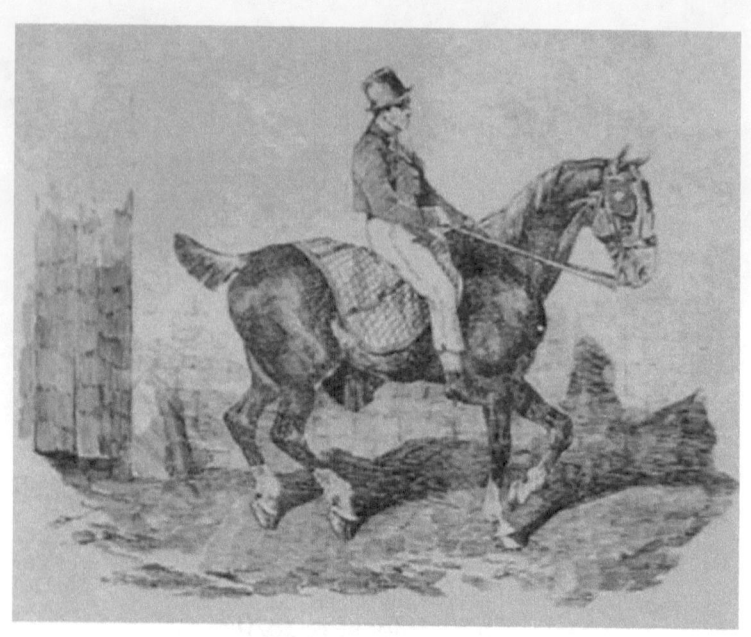

Horse carriage, 1820
Drawing

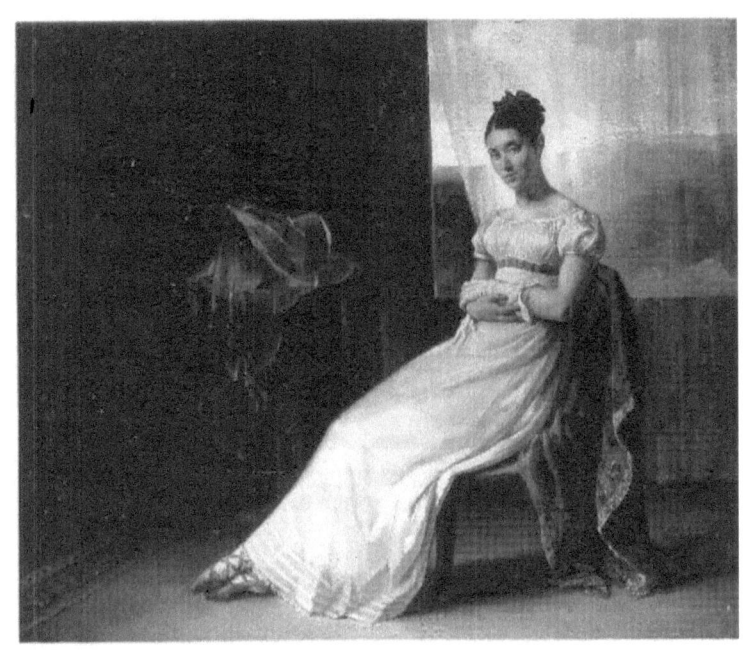

Portrait of Laura Bro, 1818-1820
Oil on canvas

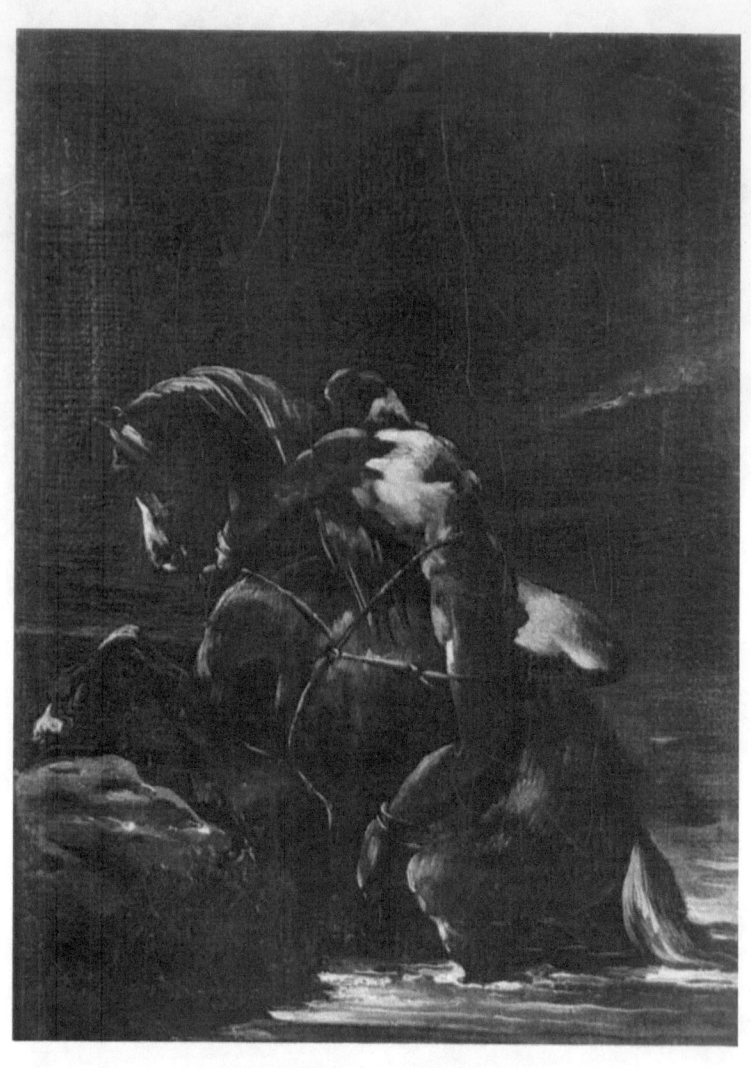

The Page Mazeppa, c.1820
Oil on canvas

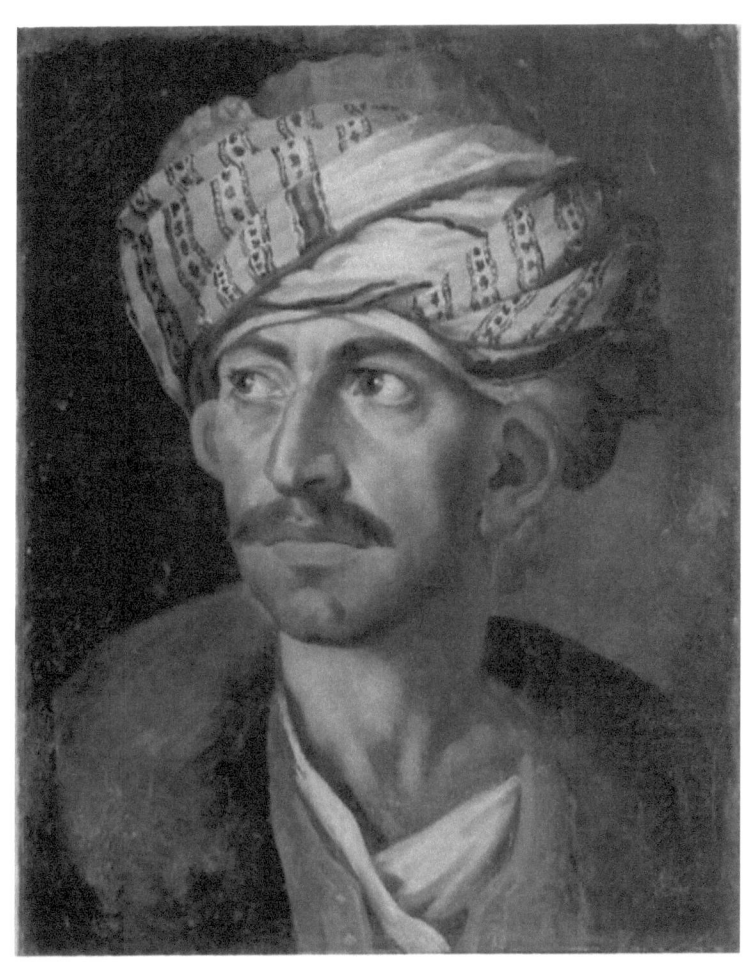

Head of an Oriental, or Portrait Presumed to be
Mustapha, 1819-1821
Oil on canvas

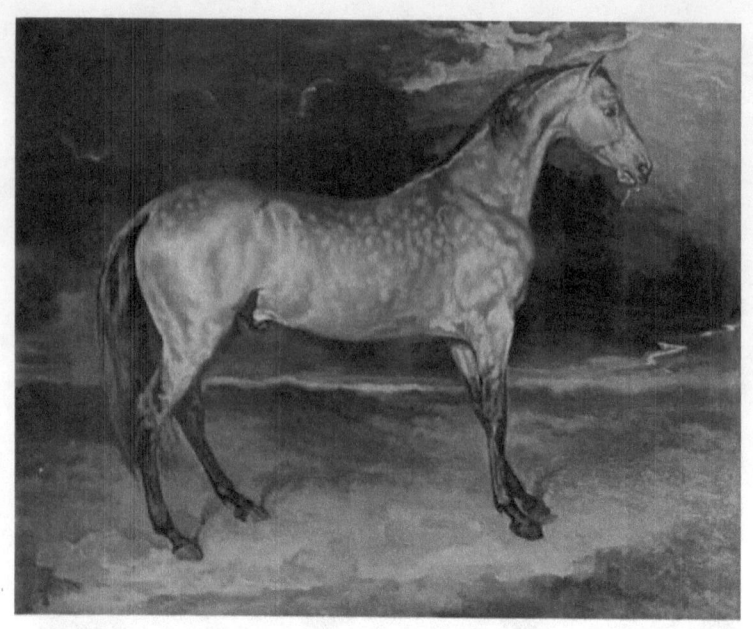

Horse in the storm, 1820-1821
Oil on canvas

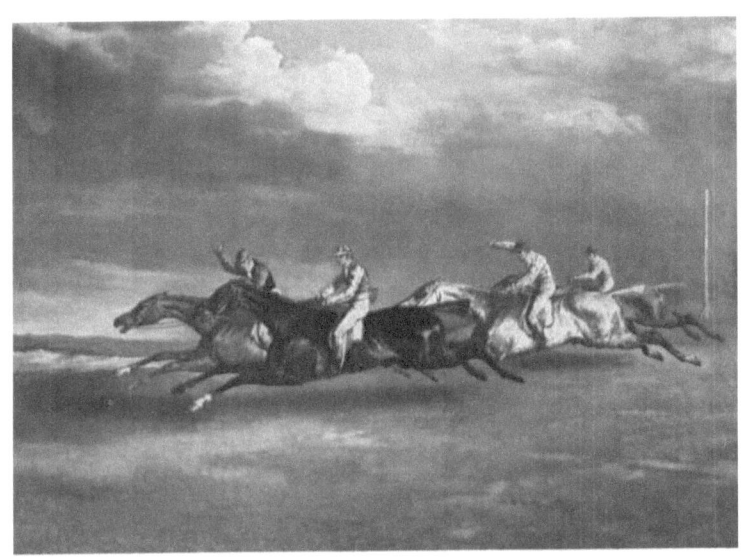

The Epsom Derby, 1821
Oil on canvas

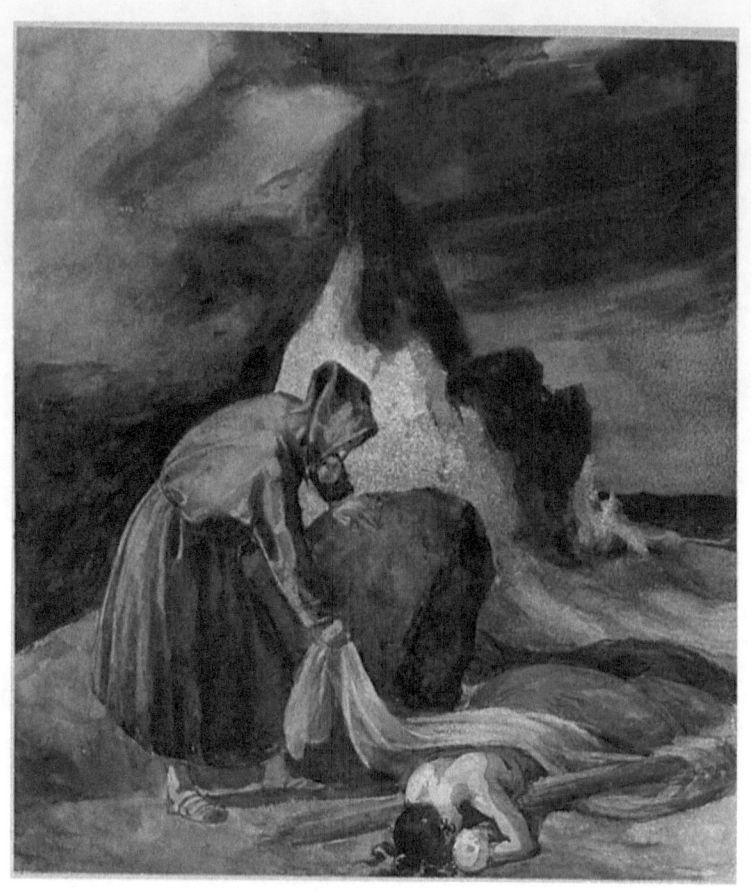

The Tempest, 1821
Watercolor

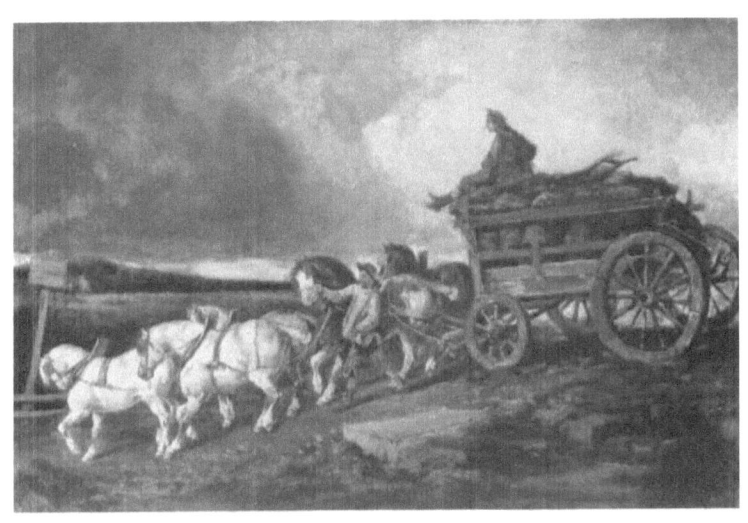

Coal cars, 1821-1822
Oil on canvas

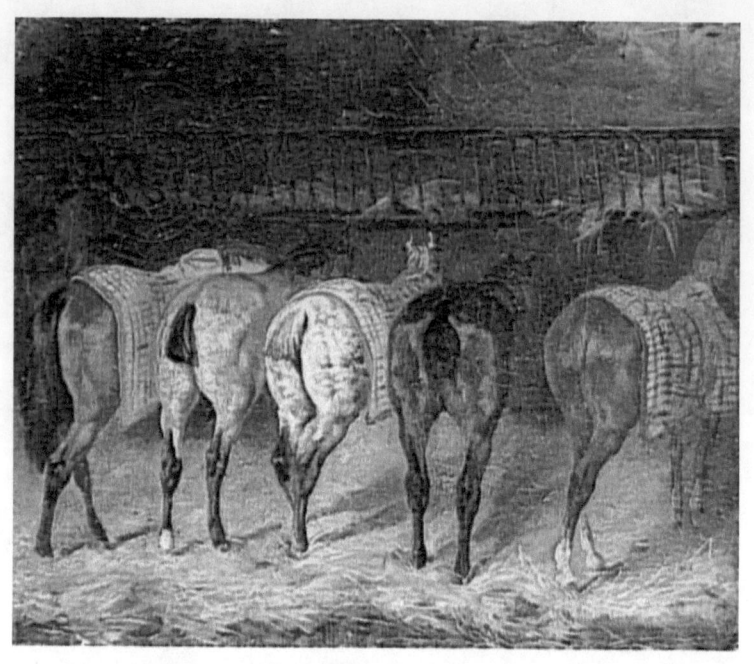

Five horses seen from behind with croupes in a stable,
1820-1822
Oil on canvas

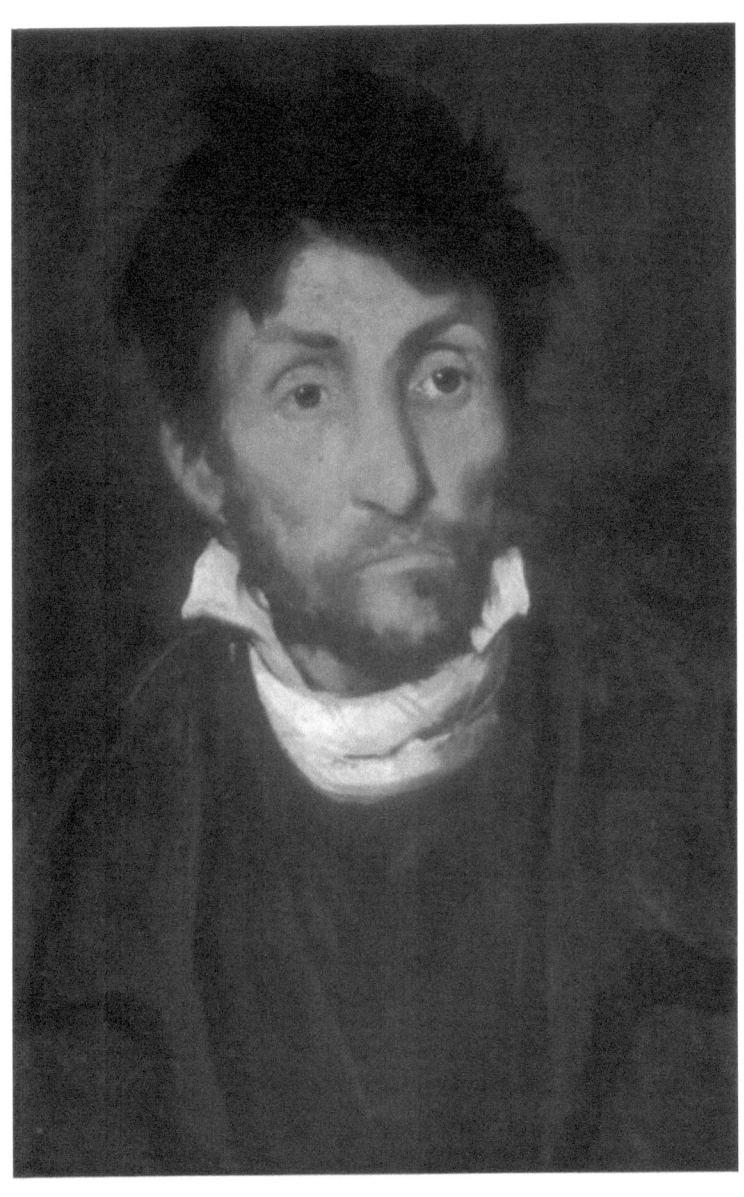

Portrait of a Kleptomaniac, 1819-1822
Oil on canvas

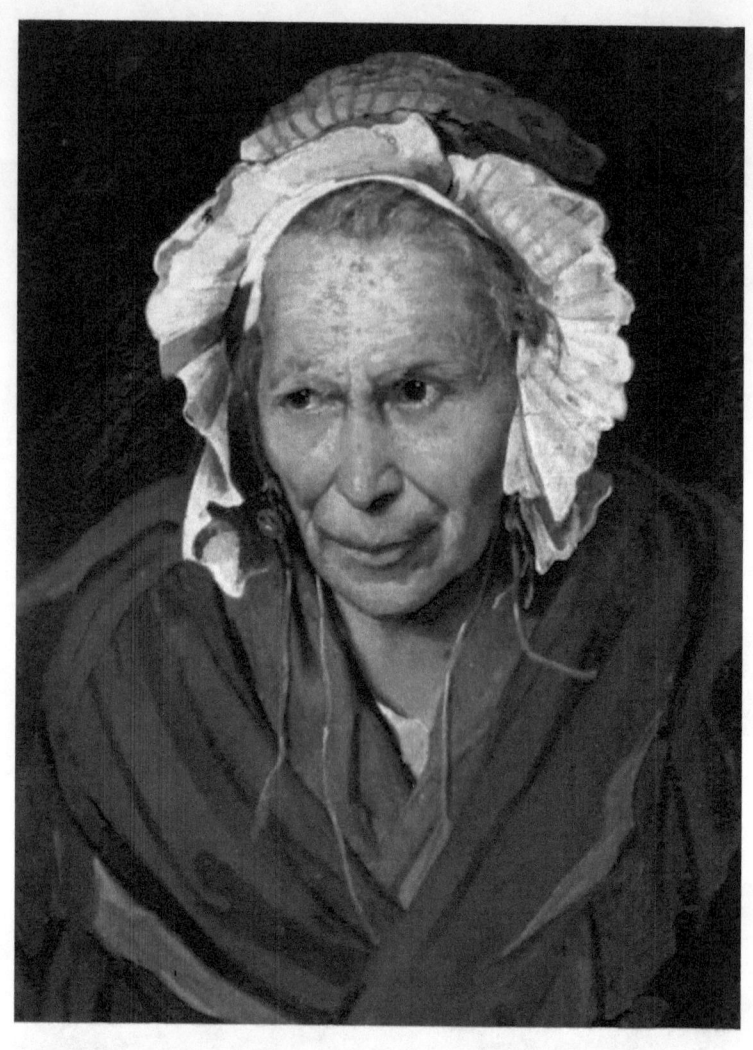

The Madwoman, or The Obsession of Envy, 1822
Oil on canvas

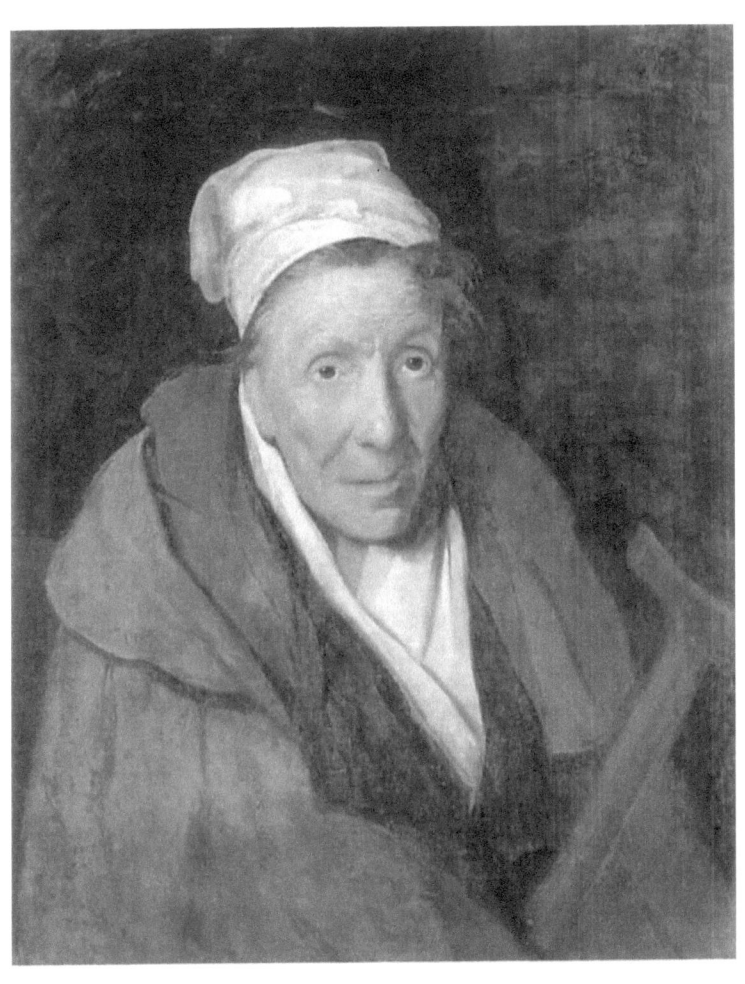

The Woman with Gambling Mania, 1819-1822
Oil on canvas

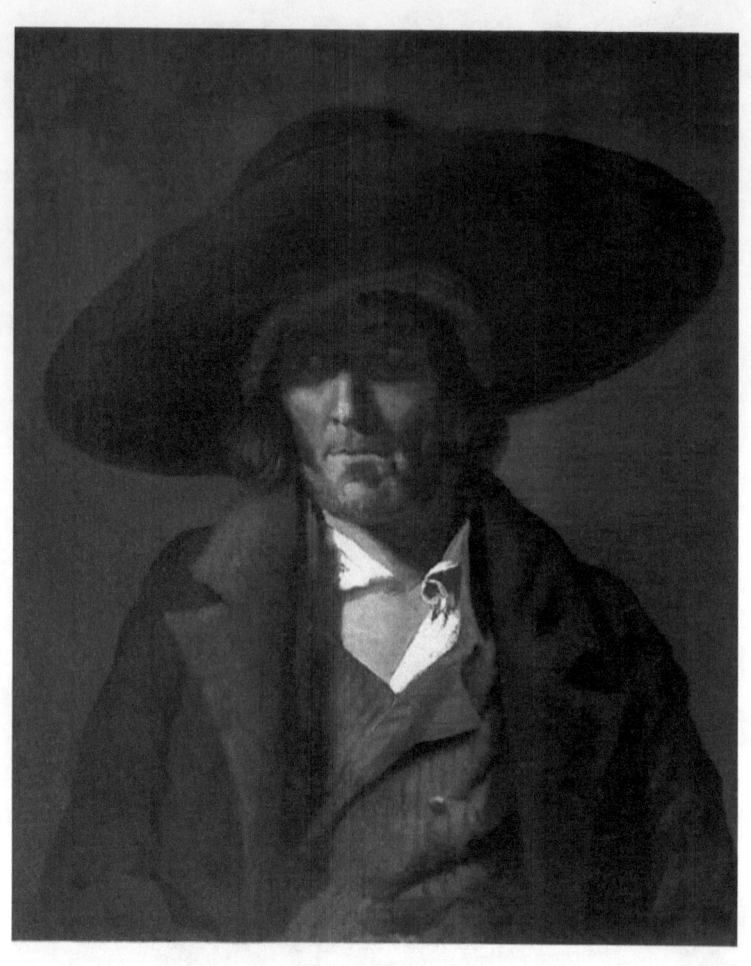

Portrait of a Man, 1822-1823
Oil on canvas

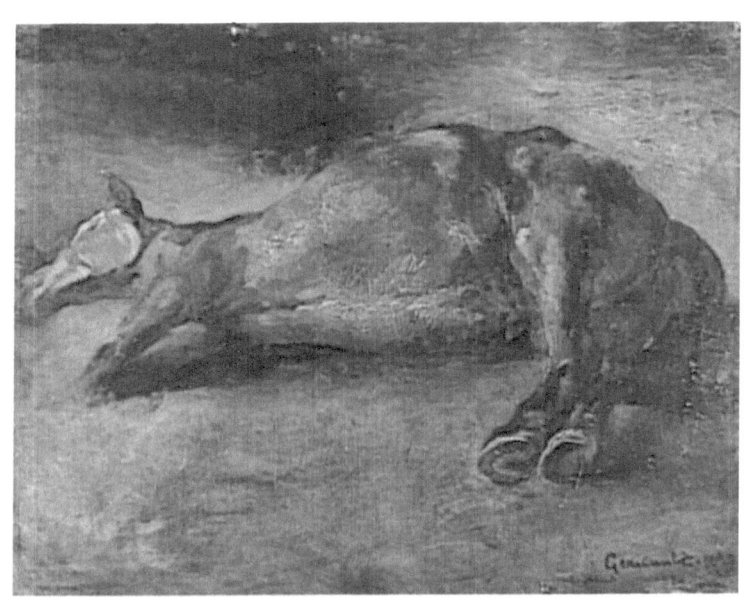

Study for Dead horse, 1823
Oil on canvas

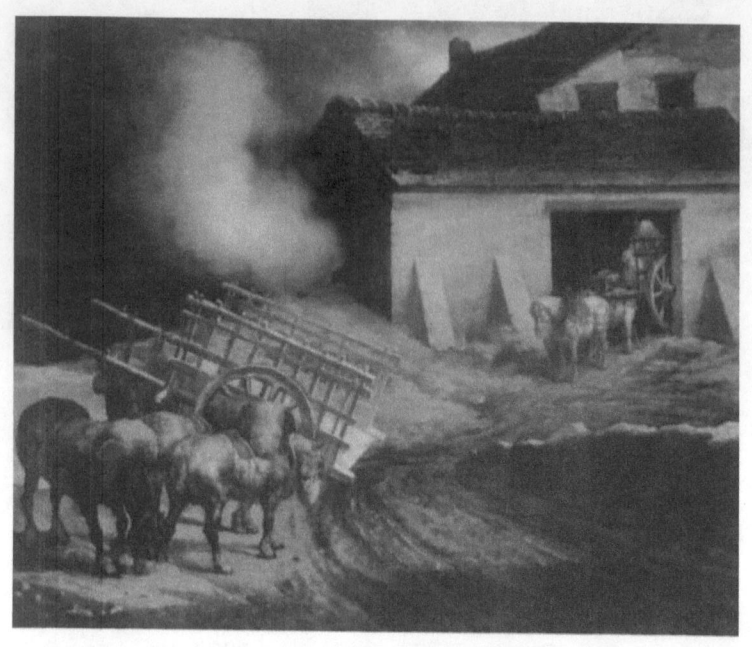

The Plaster Kiln, 1822-1823
Oil on canvas

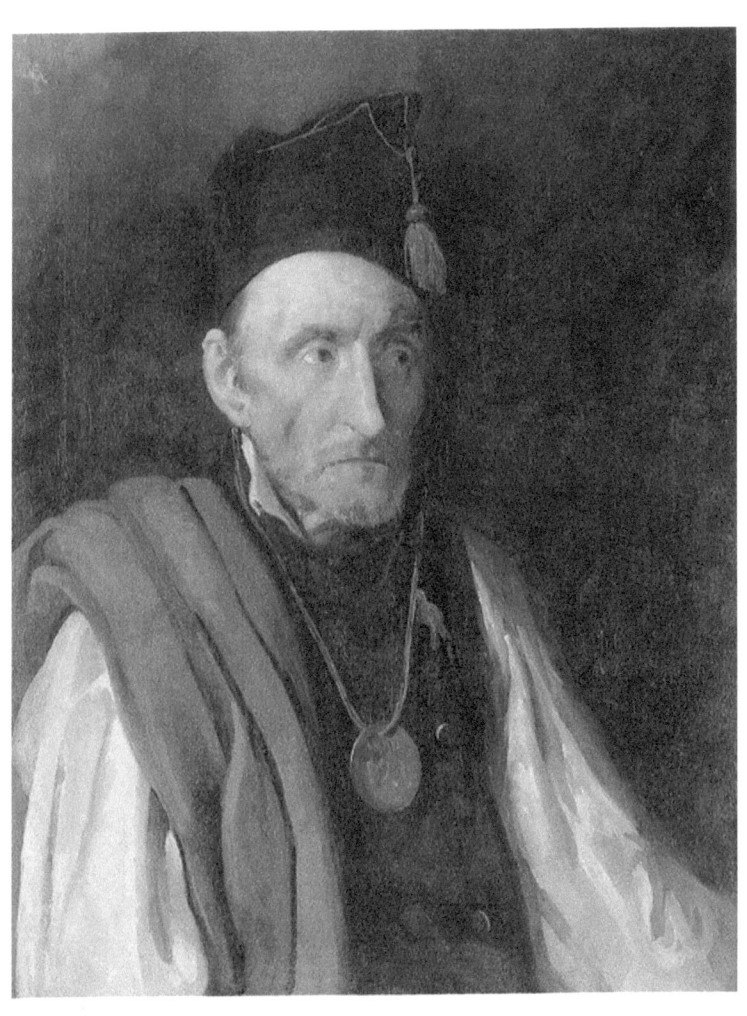

The Insane, 1822-1823
Oil on canvas

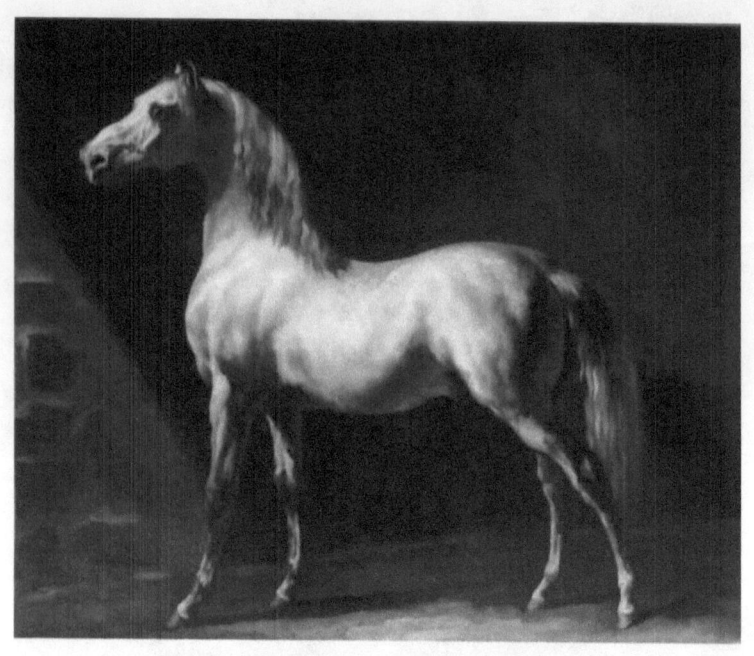

Study of a Dapple Grey, 1812-1824
Oil on canvas

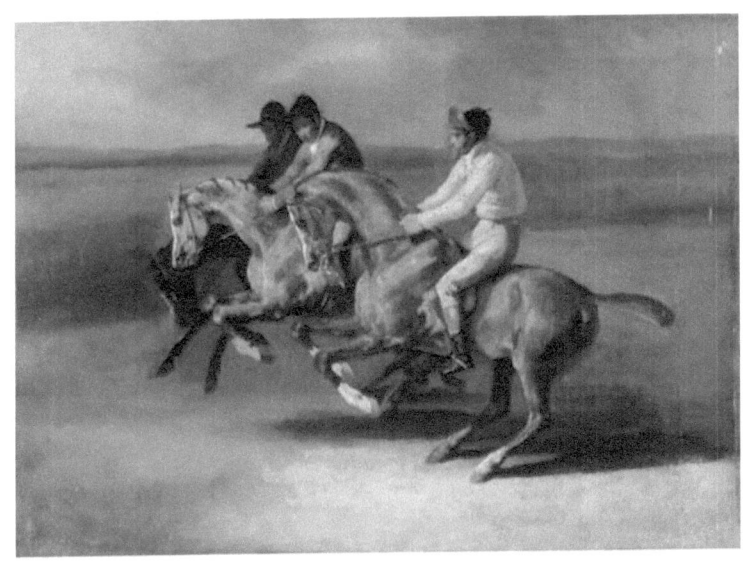

The Horse Race, 1820-1824
Oil on canvas

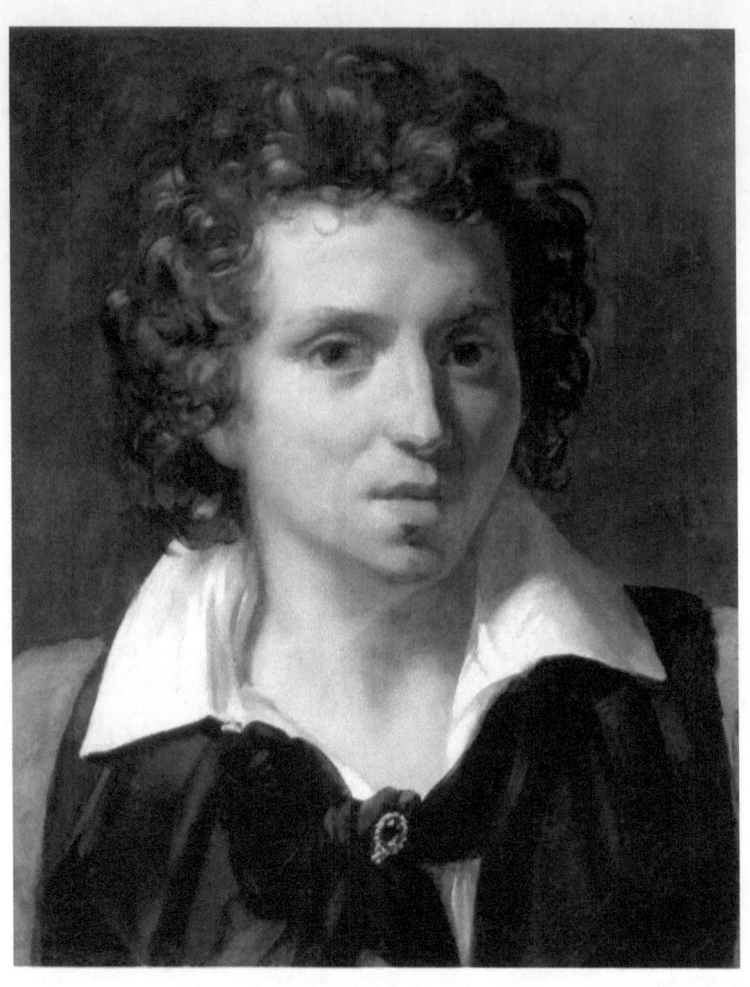

A Portrait Of A Young Man
Oil on canvas

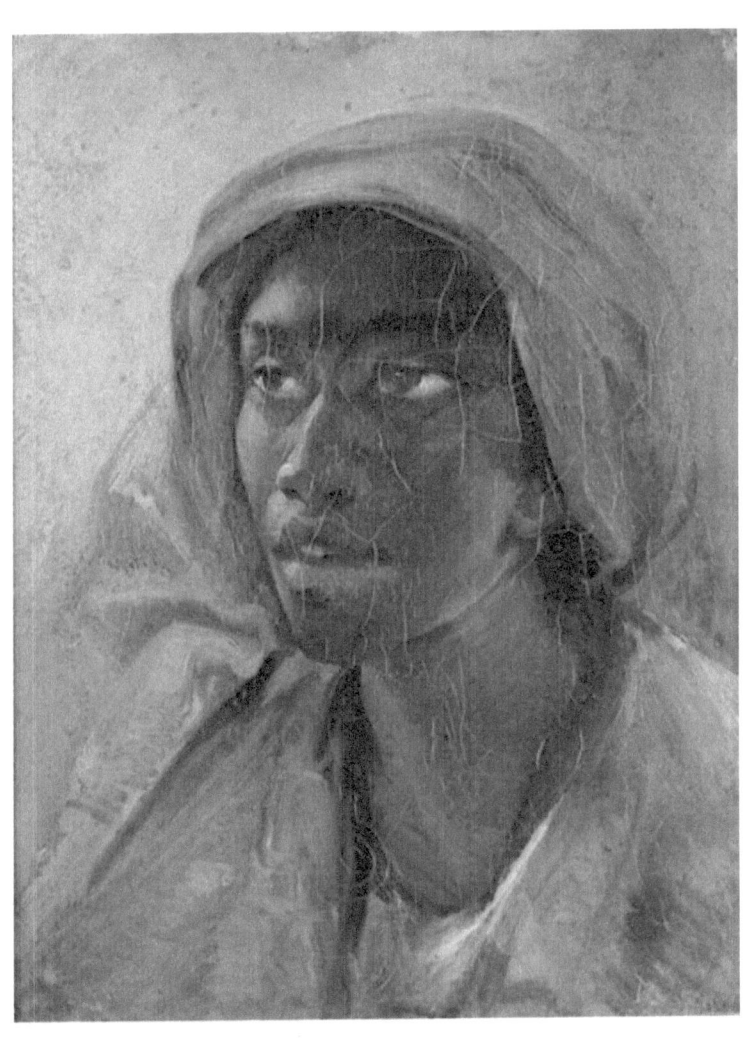

A Young Negro Woman
Oil on canvas

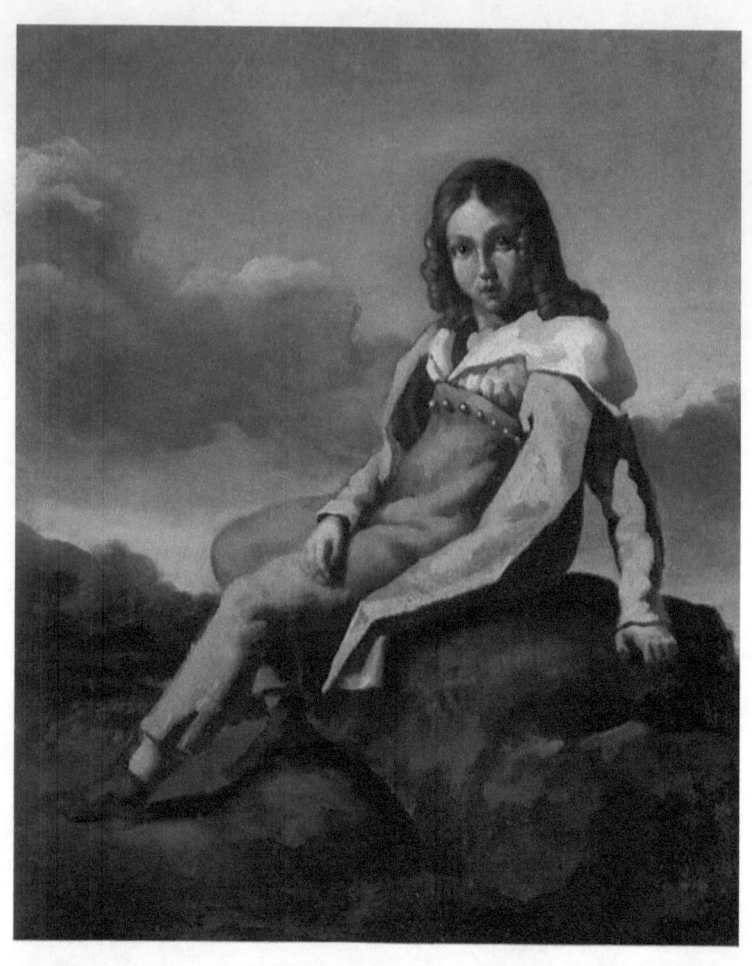

Alfred Dedreux as a Child
Oil on canvas

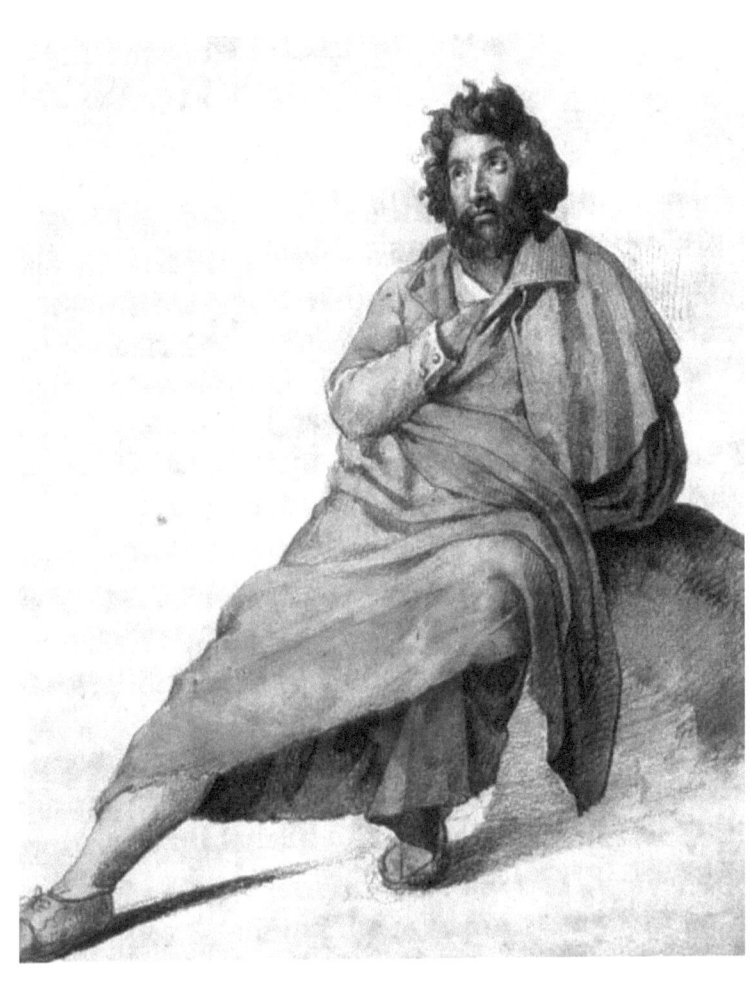

An Italian montagnard

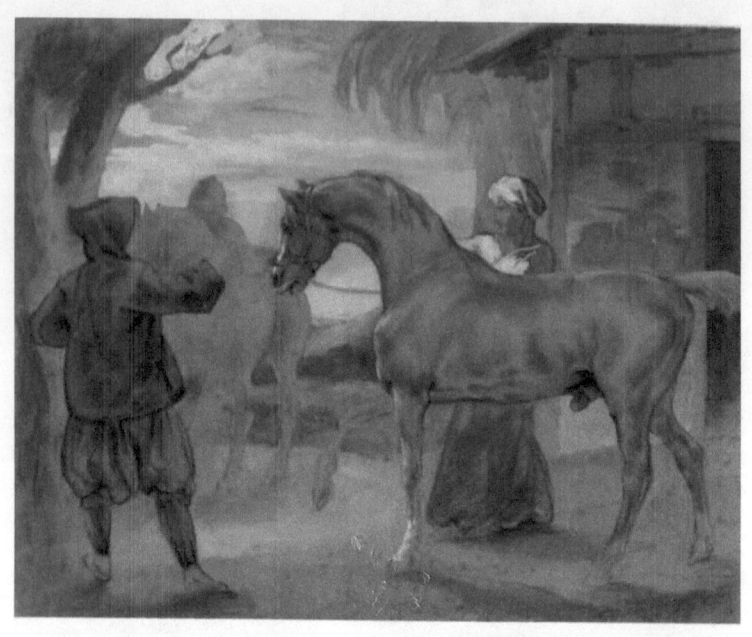

Arabian Stallion led by two Arabians to breed
Watercolor

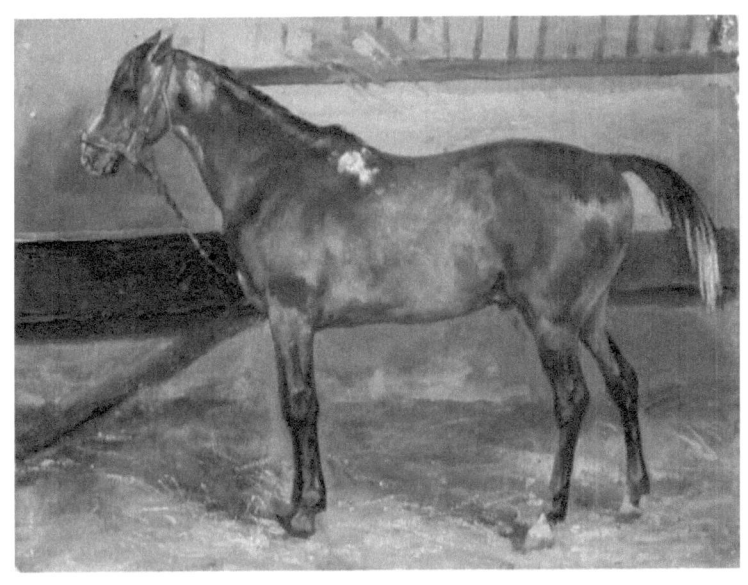

Brown Horse in the Stalls
Oil on canvas

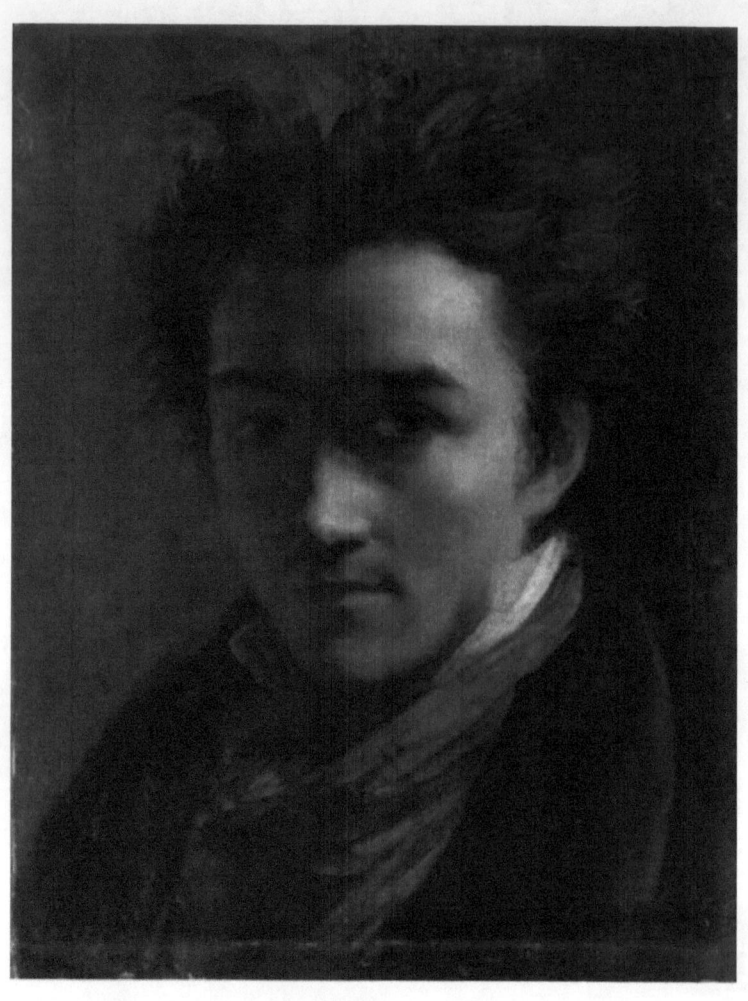

Colin Alexander, painter
Oil on canvas

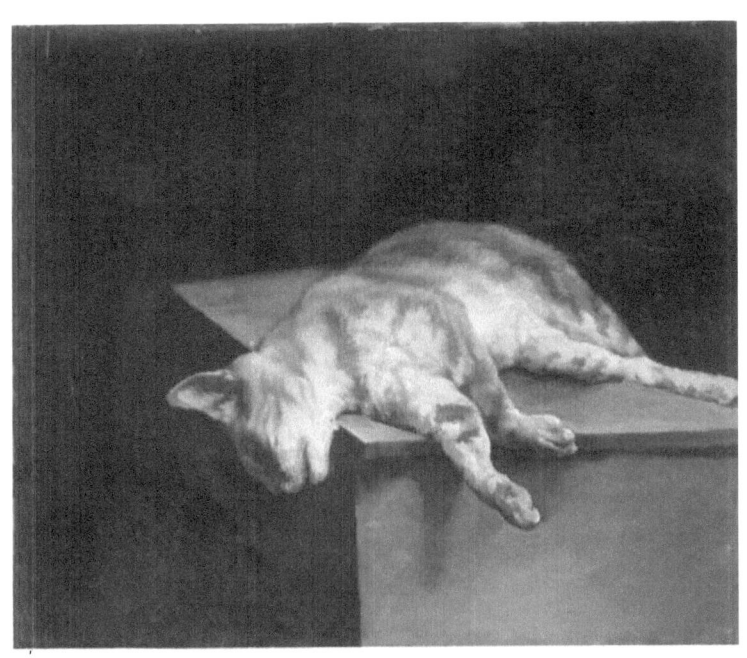

Dead Cat
Oil on canvas

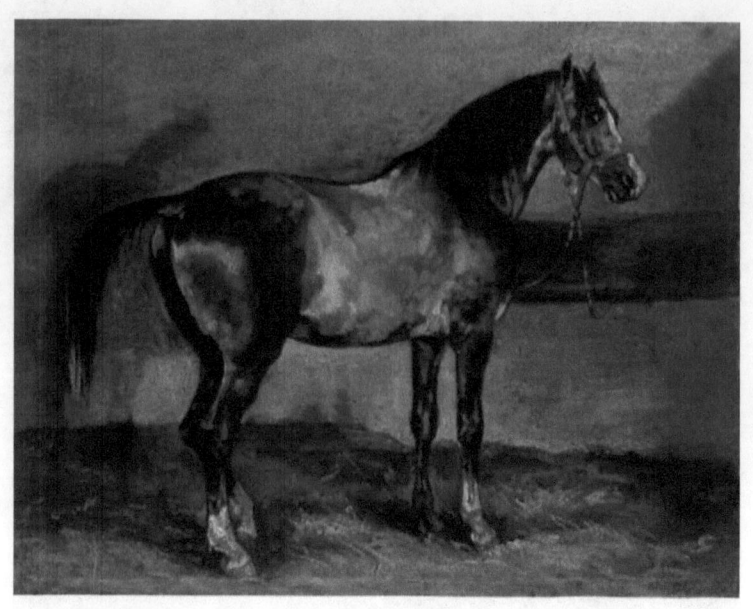

Gray horse rack,
Oil on canvas

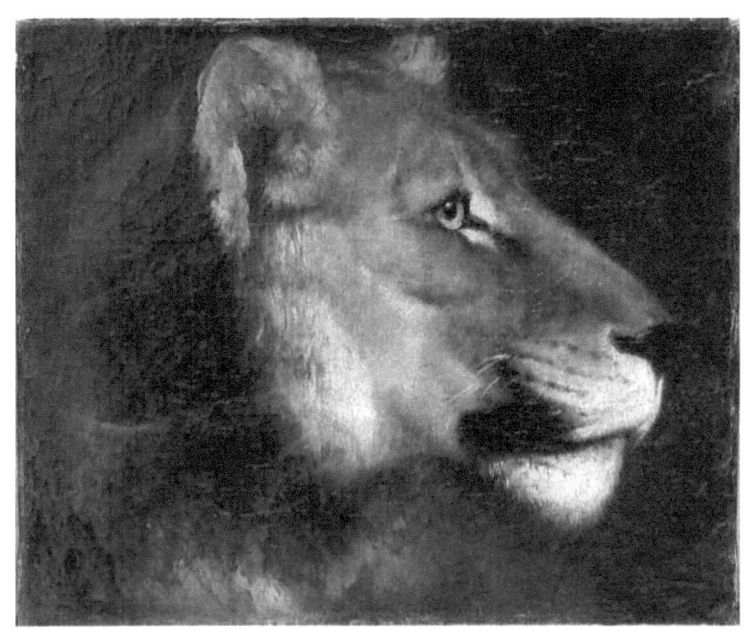

Head of lioness, Oil on canvas

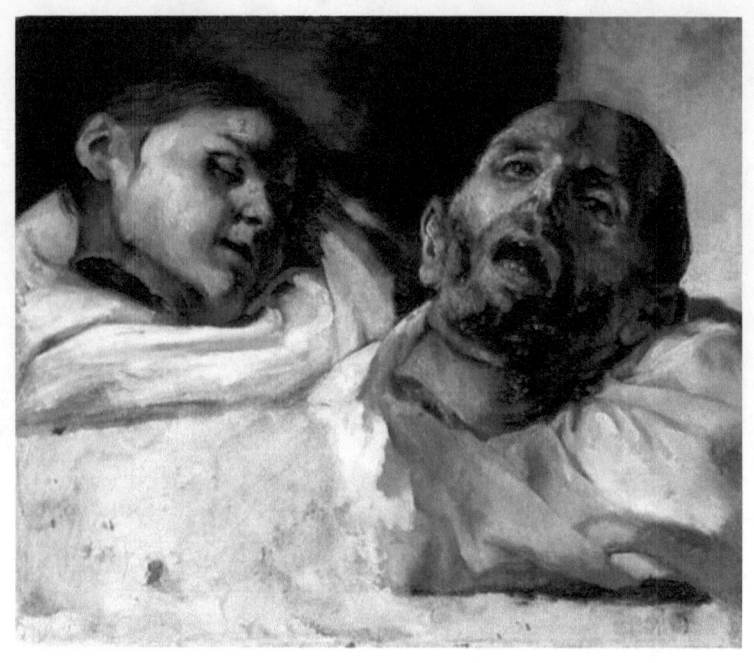

Heads of Torture Victims (study for The Raft of the
Medusa)
Oil on canvas

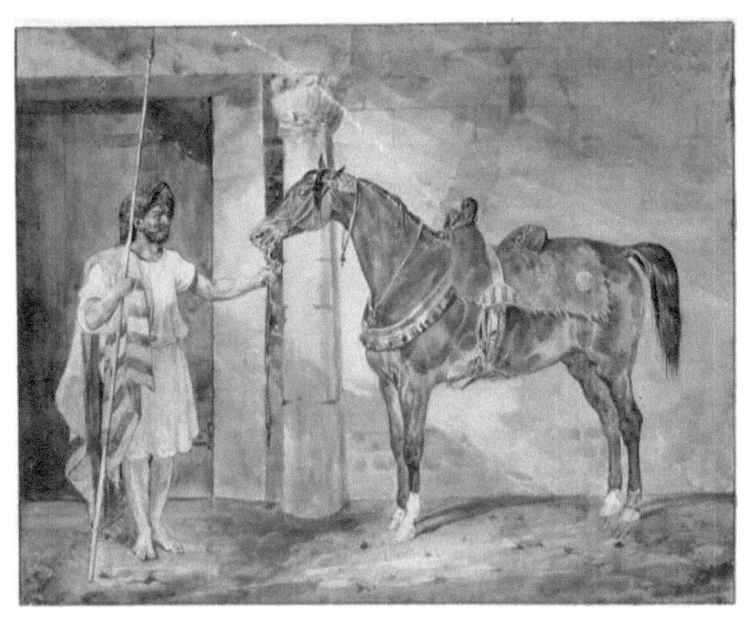

Horse (Eastern)
Watercolor

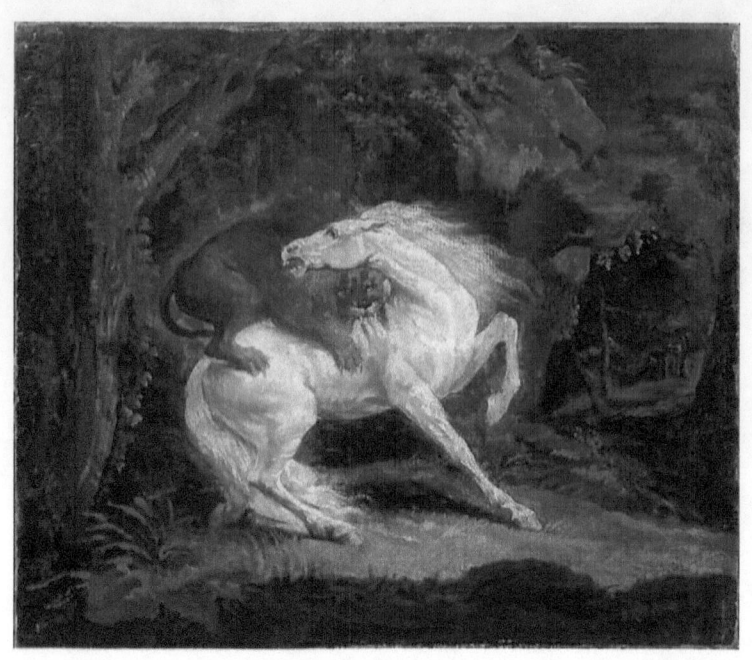

Horse attacked by a lion
Oil on canvas

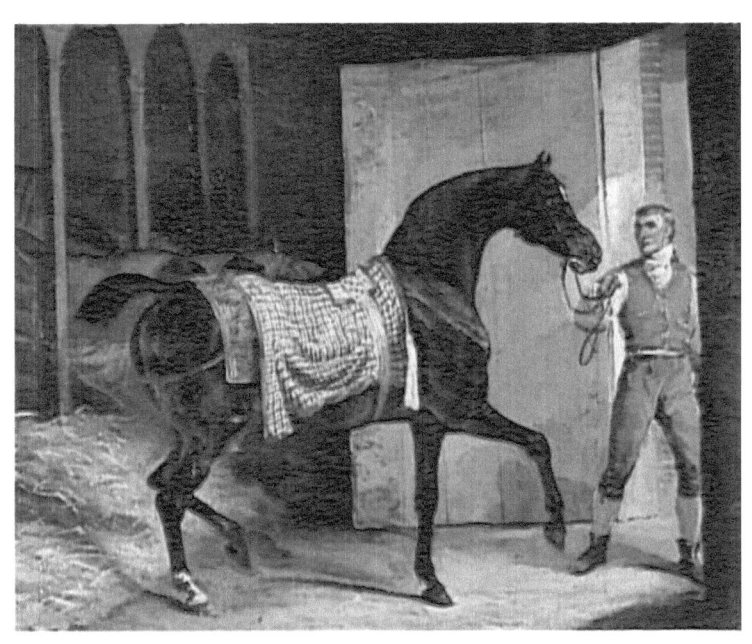

Horse leaving a Stable
Oil on canvas

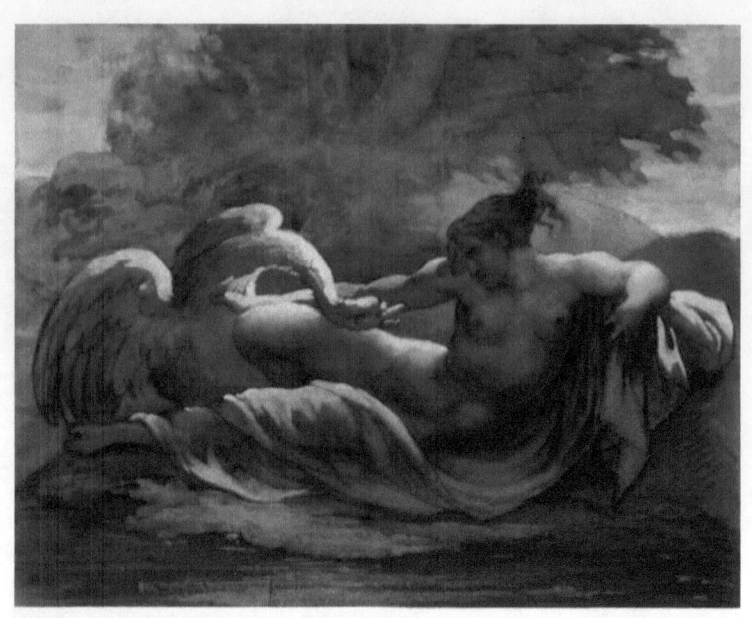

Leda and the Swan
Watercolor

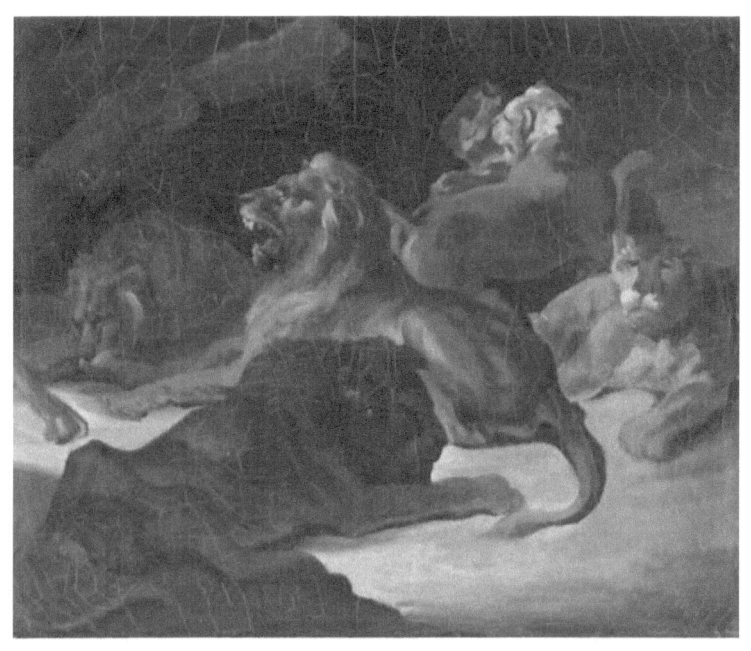

Lying Lions
Oil

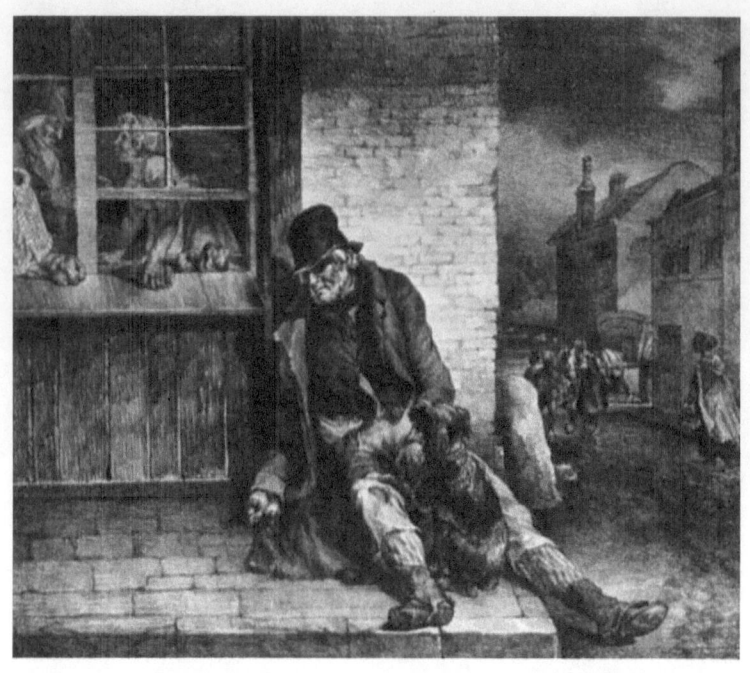

Man on the street
Engraving

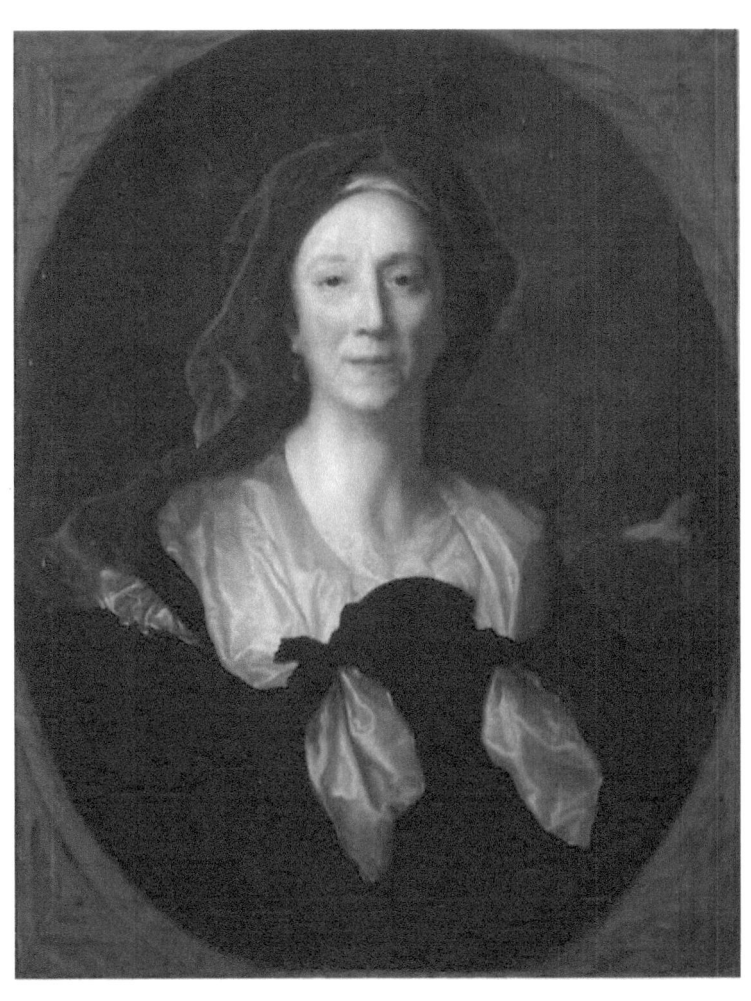

Maria Serre
Oil on canvas

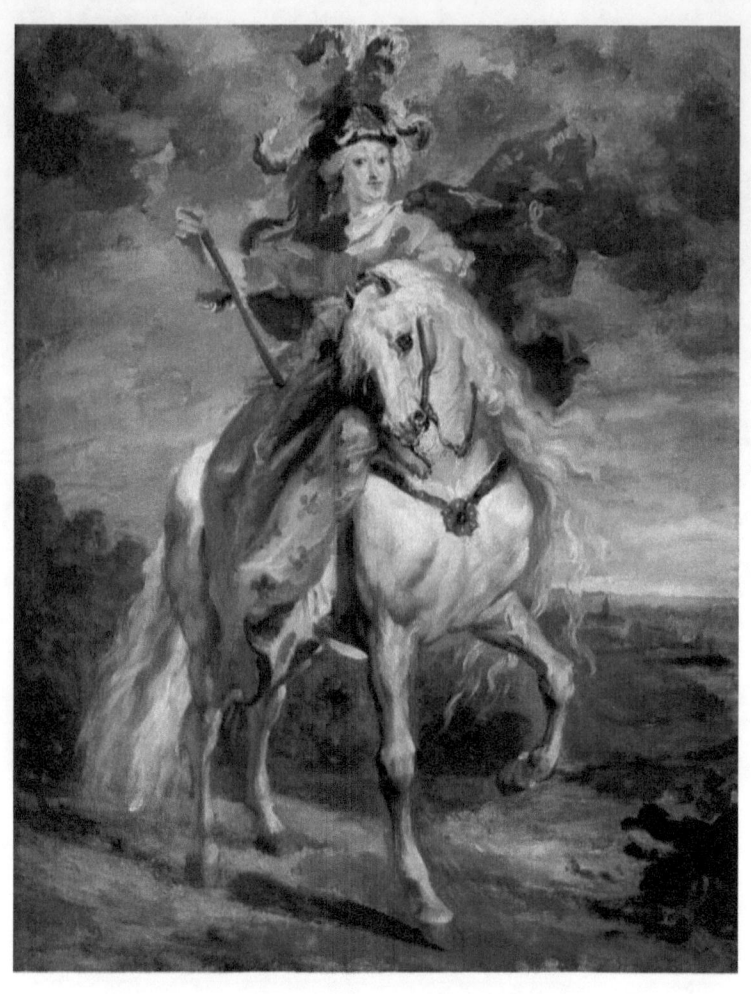

Marie de Medici at Pont-de-Ce
Oil on canvas

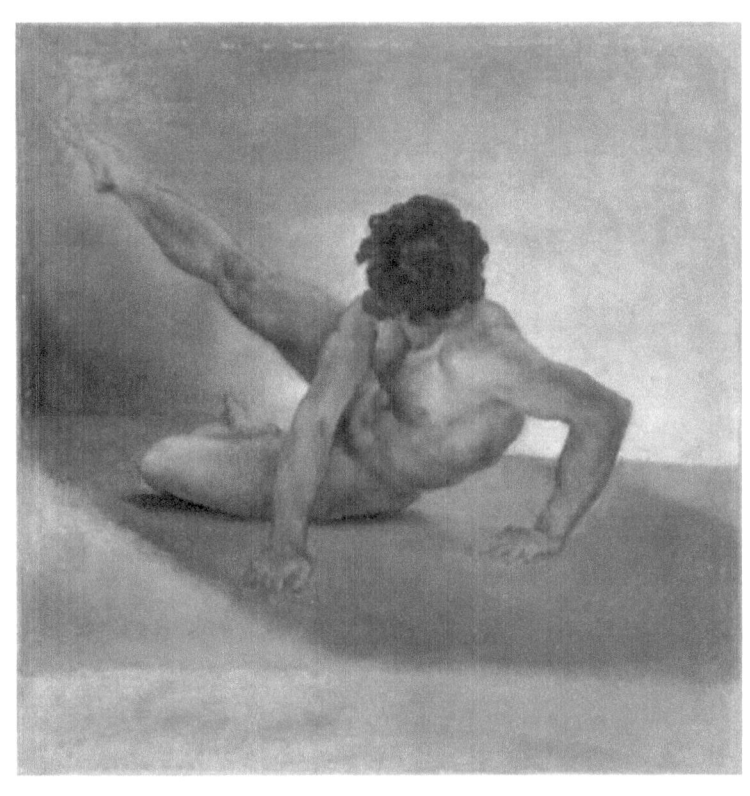

Naked man reversed on the ground
Oil

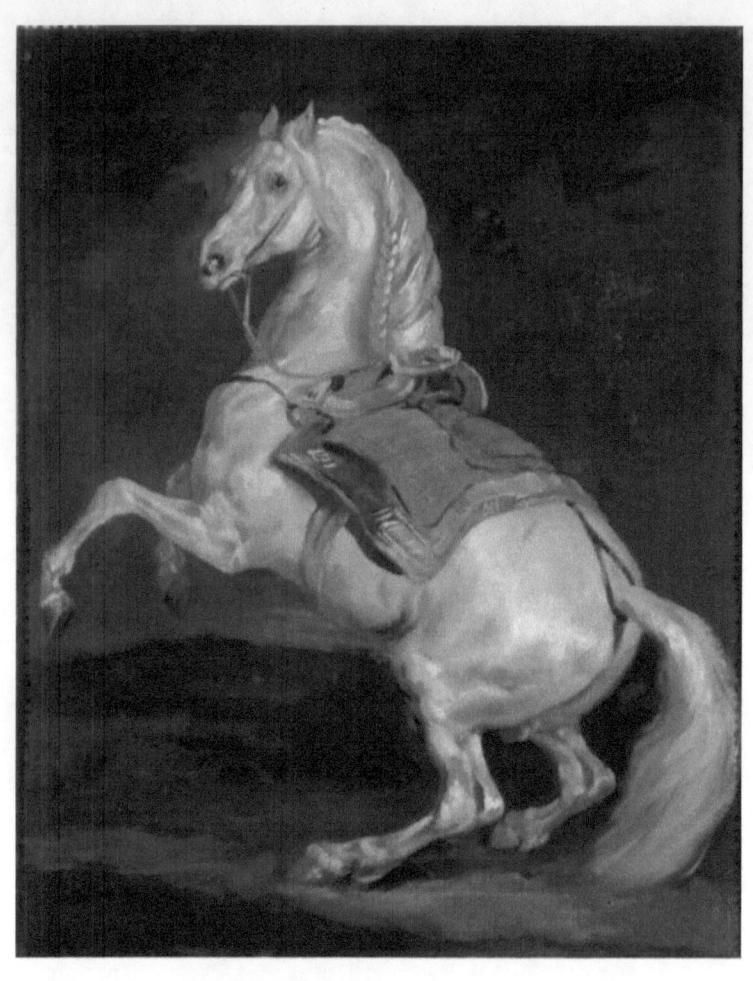

Napoleon's Stallion, Tamerlan
Oil on canvas

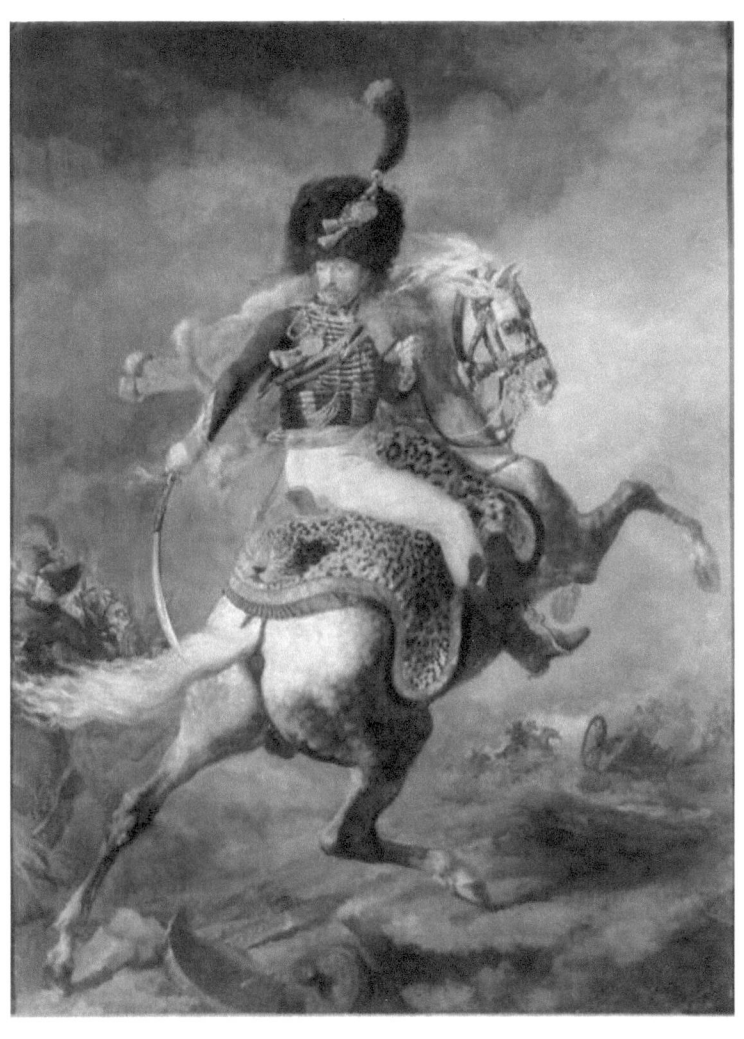

Officer of the Chasseurs charging on horseback
Oil on panel

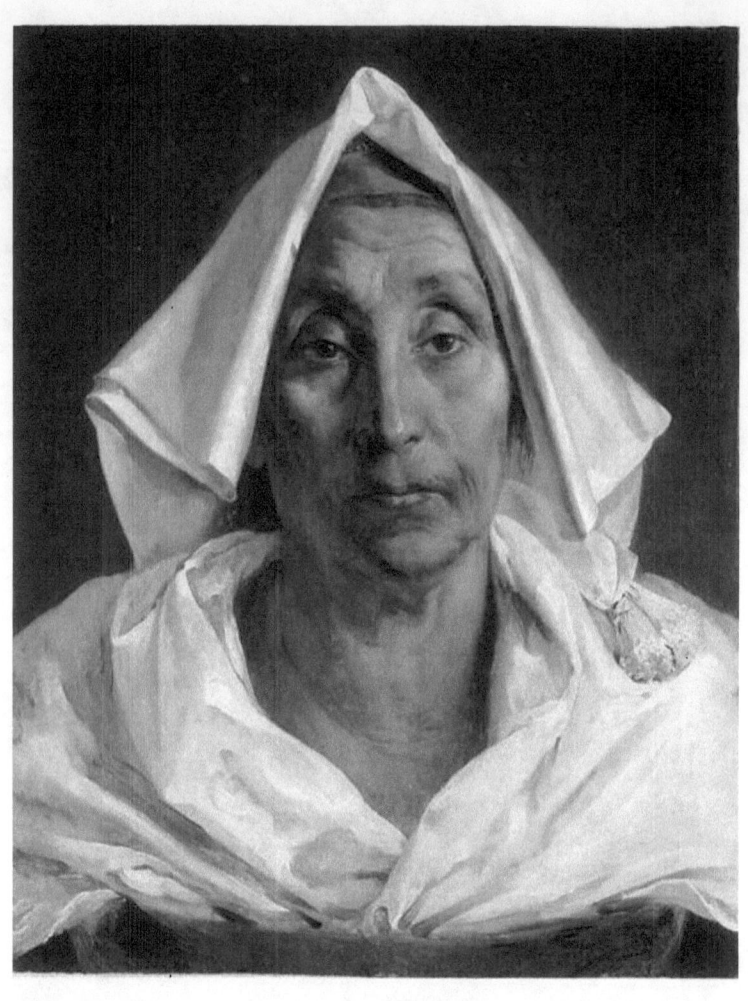

Old Italian peasant
Oil on canvas

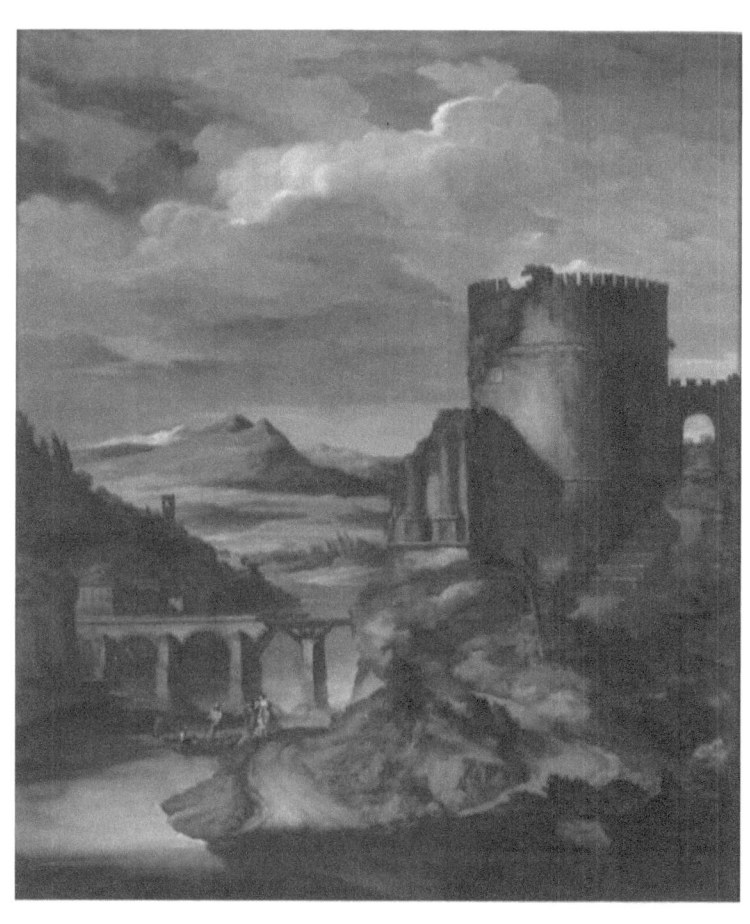

Paysage Classique: Matin
Oil on canvas

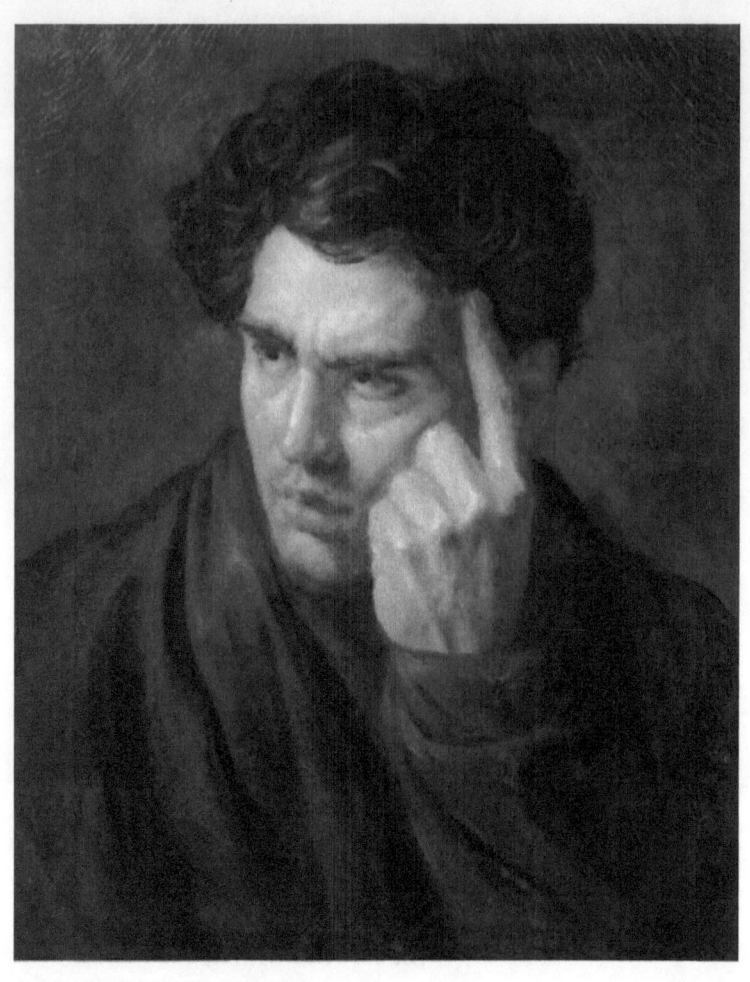

Portrait of Lord Byron
Oil on canvas

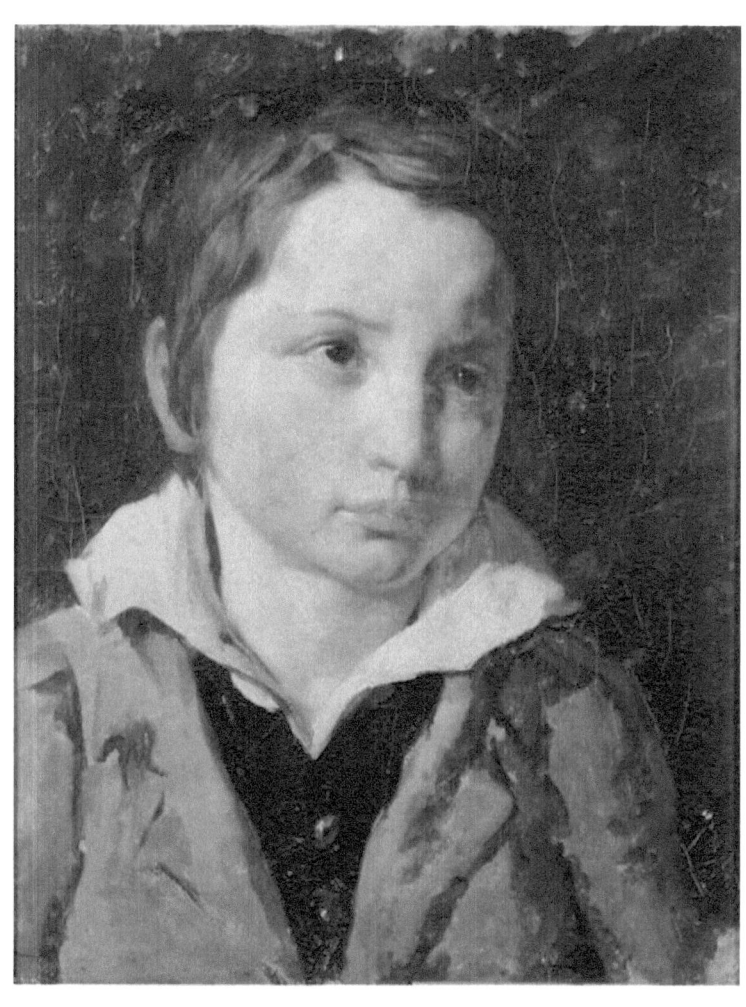

Portrait of young boy, probably Olivier Bro
Oil on canvas

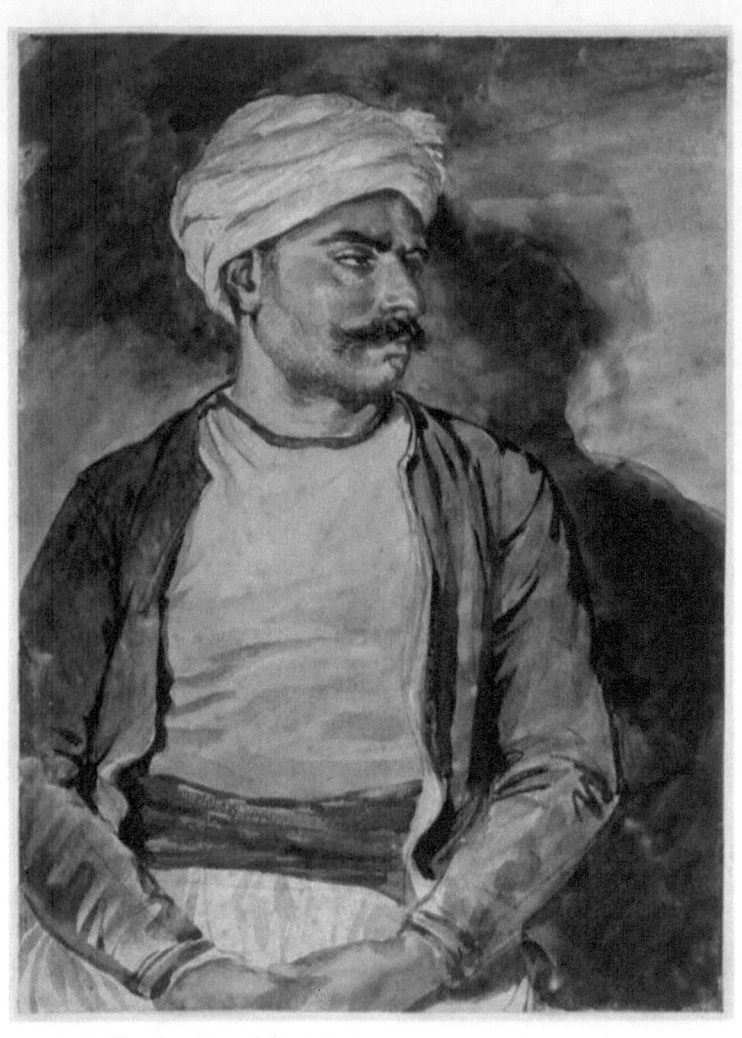

Portrait of Mustapha
Watercolor

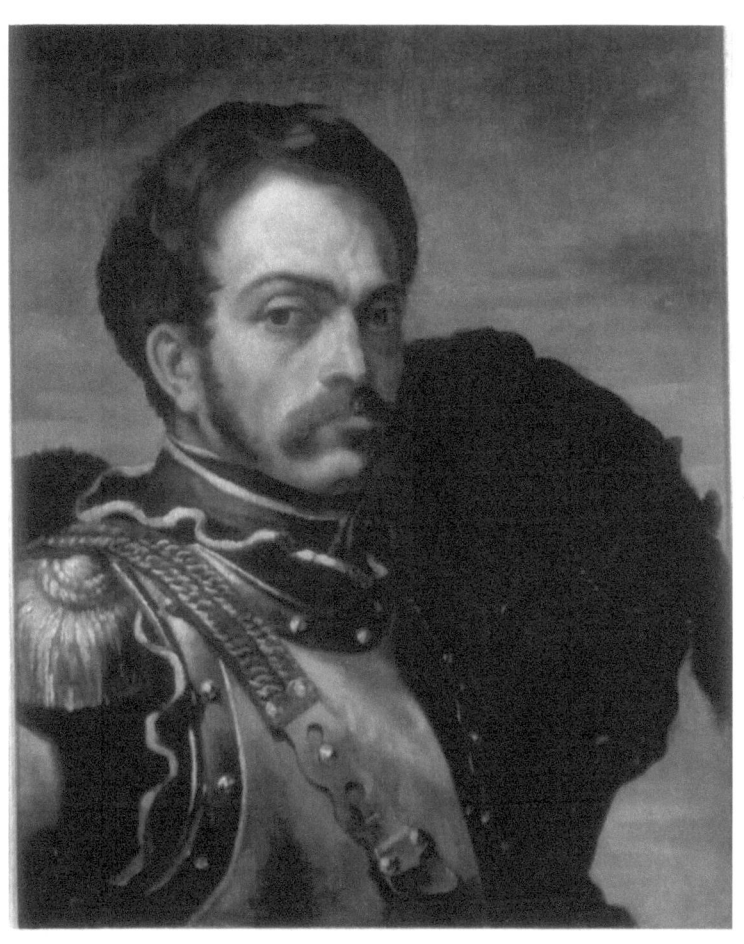

Portrait of Rifleman
Oil on canvas

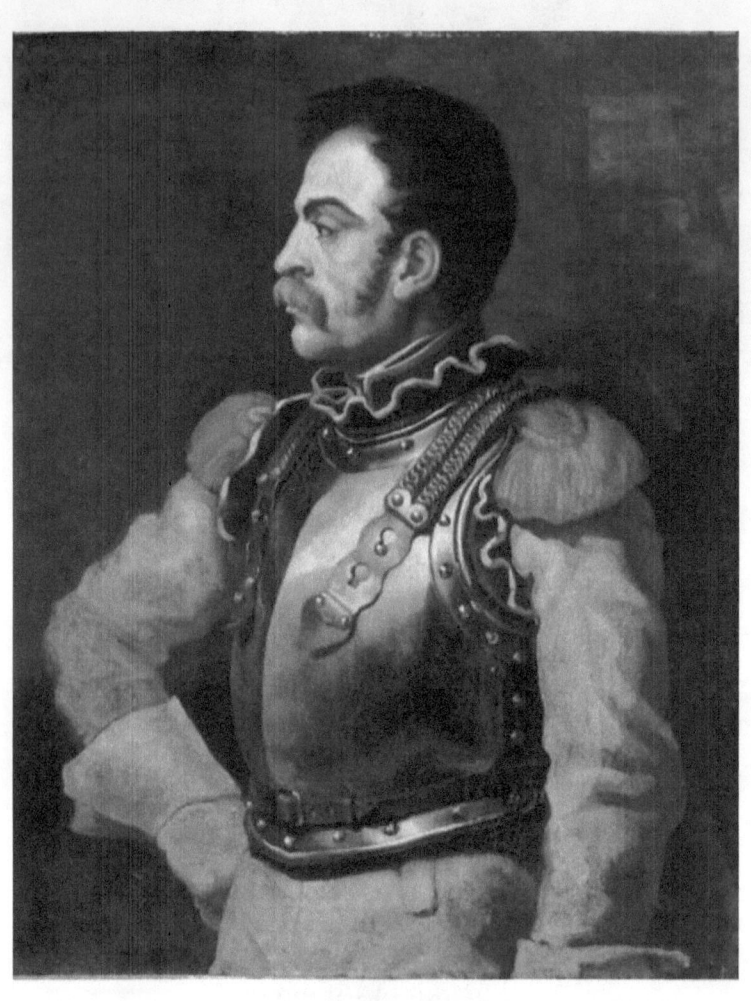

Rifleman
Oil on canvas

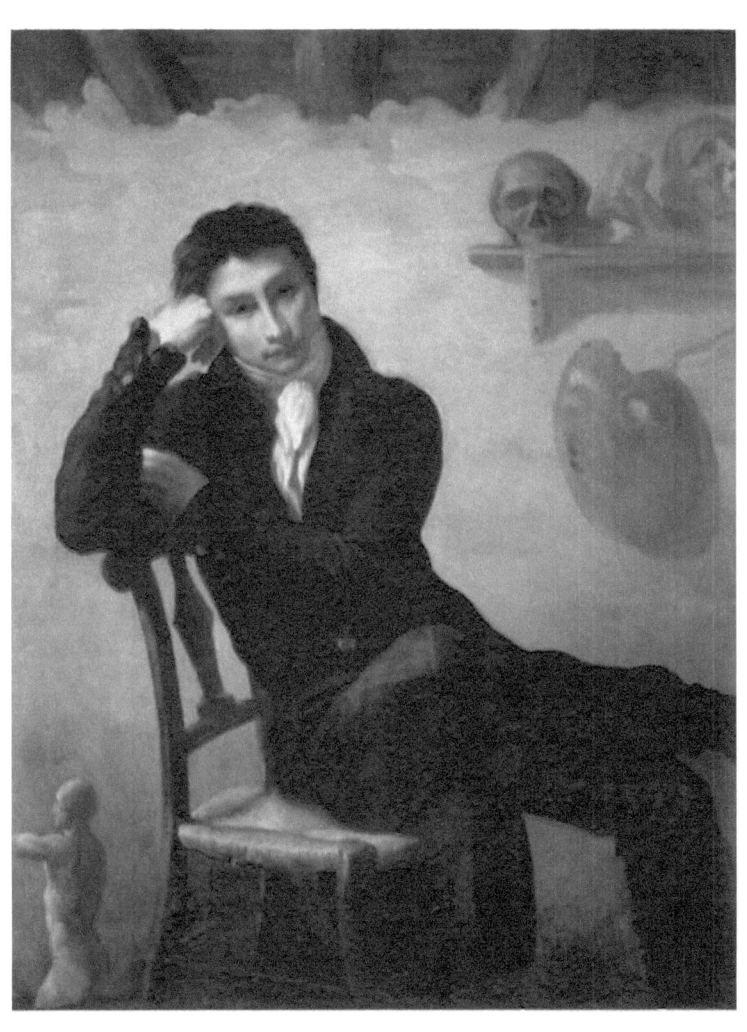

Self-Portrait
Oil on canvas

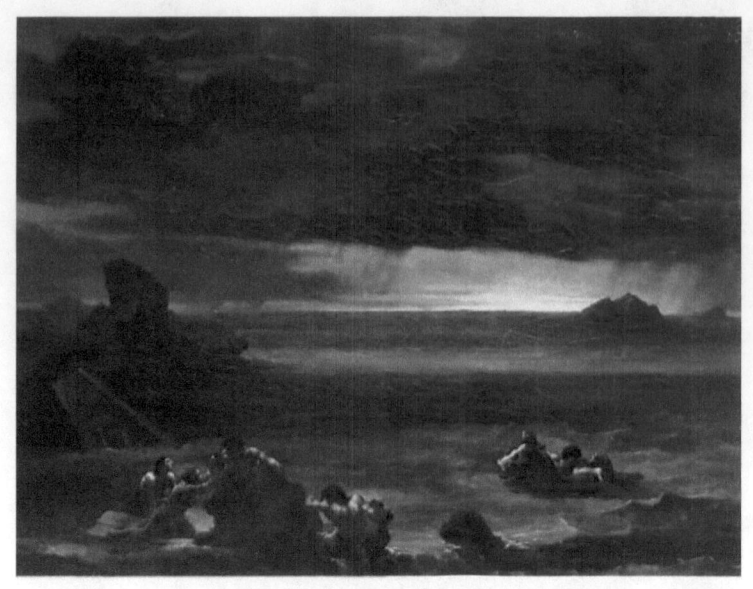

Scene of the Deluge
Oil

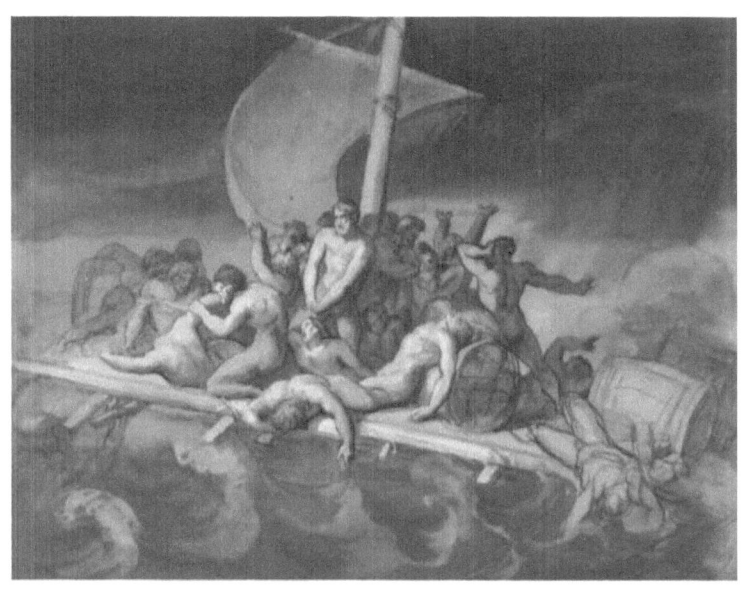

Scene of Cannibalism for The Raft of the Medusa
Watercolor

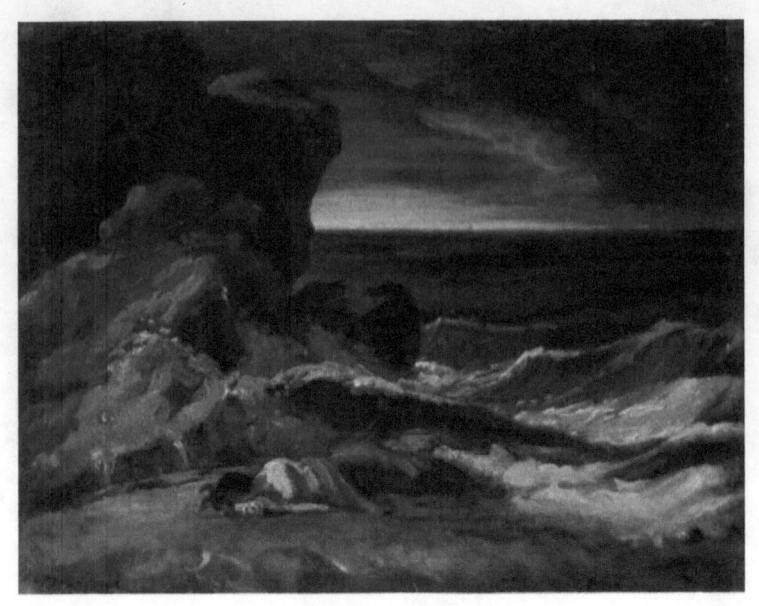

Shipwreck
Oil on canvas

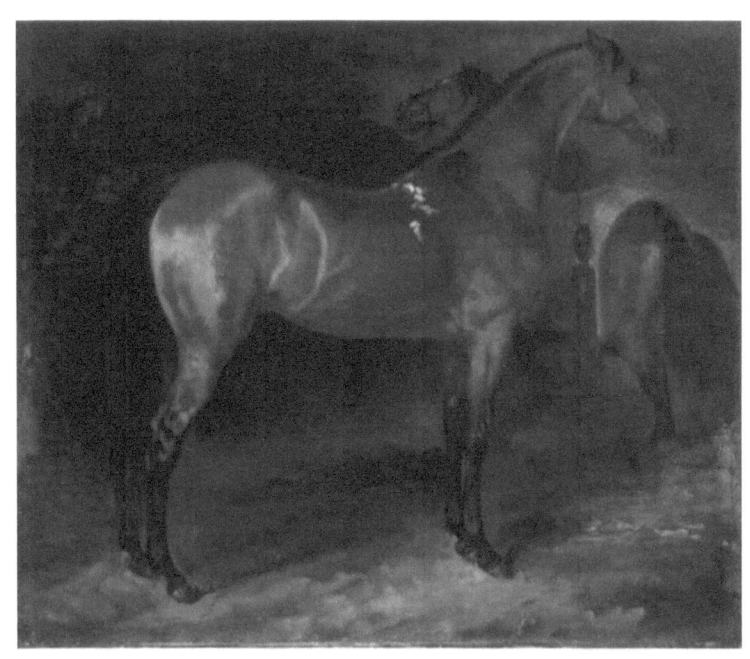

Spanish horse in a stable
Oil on canvas

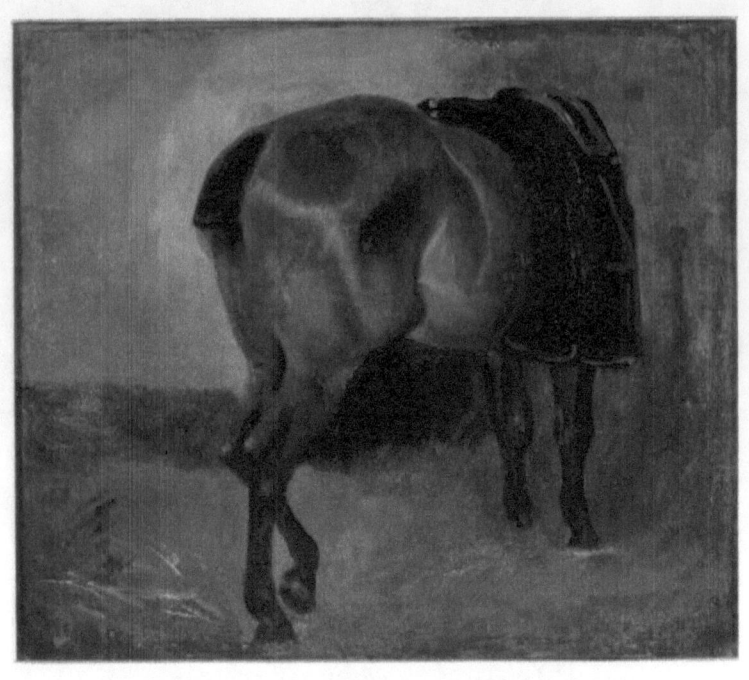

Study for Bay horse seen from behind
Oil on canvas

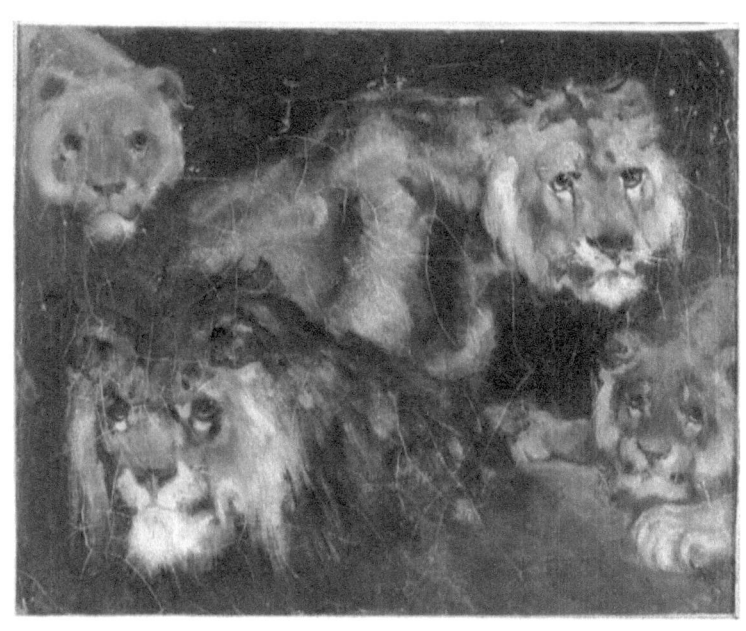

Study for Four Lions
Oil on canvas

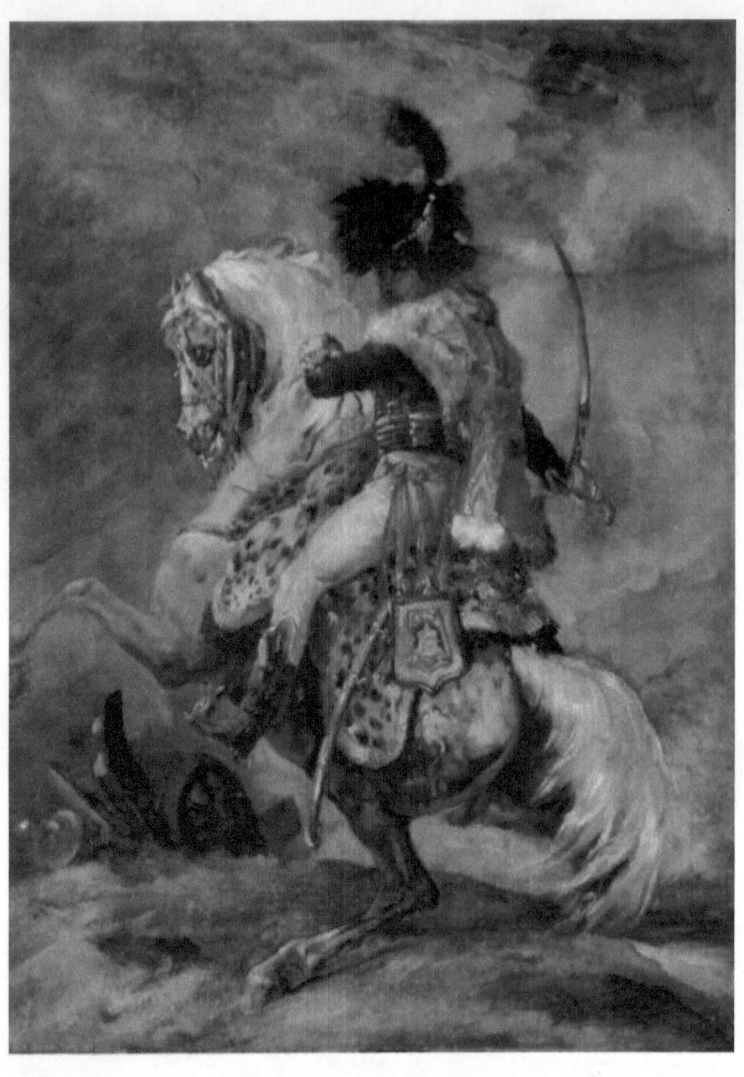

Study for Officer of Chasseurs of the Imperial Guard
Oil on canvas

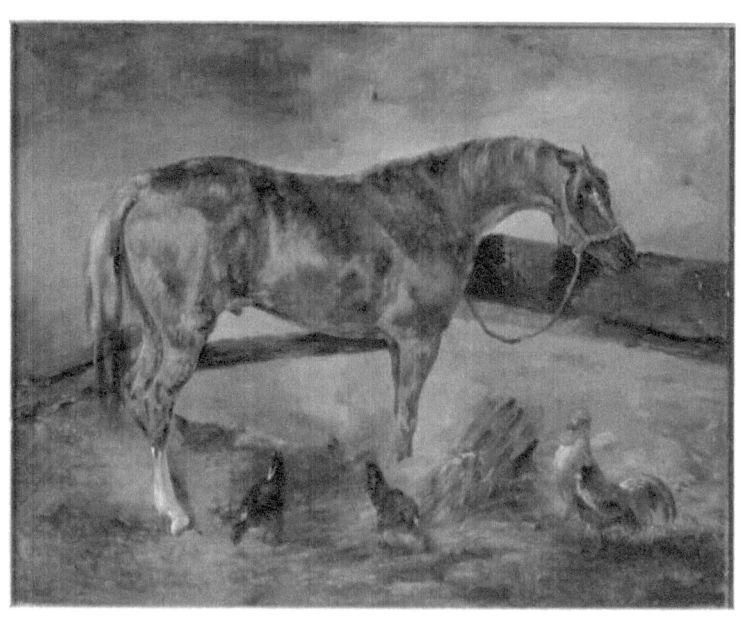

Study for Horse turned right with three hens and a
rooster
Oil on canvas

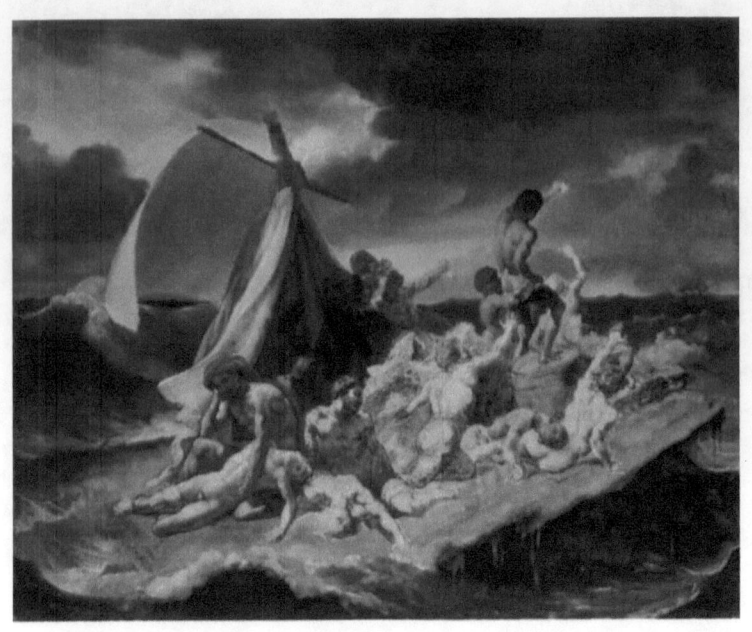

Study for The Raft of the Medusa

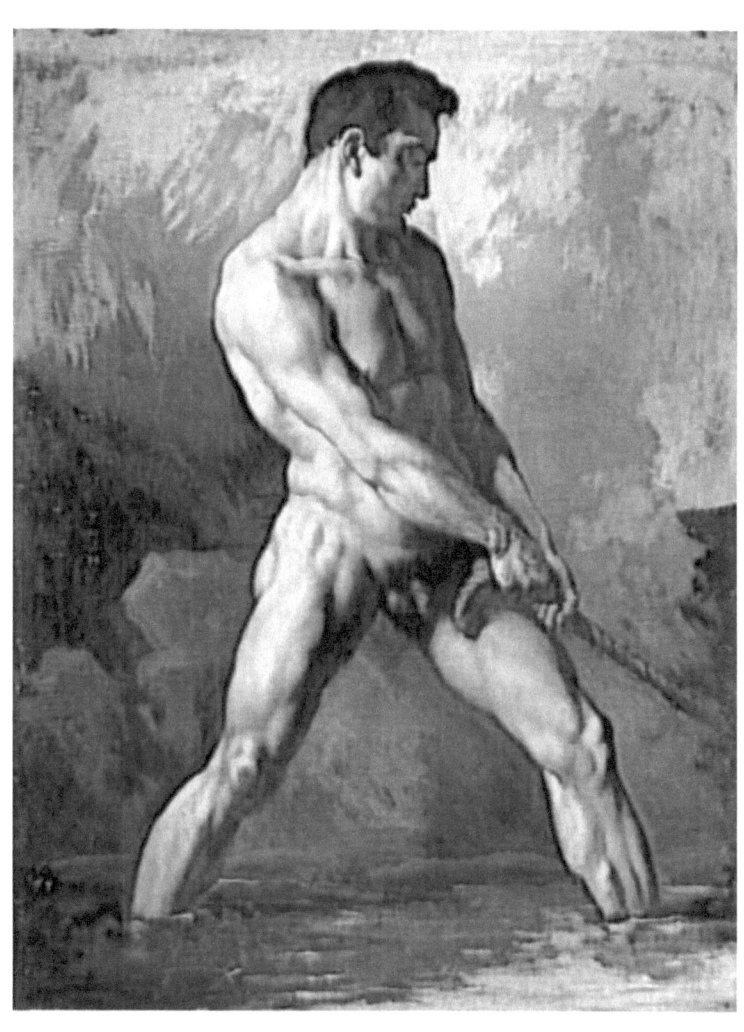

Study of a Male Nude

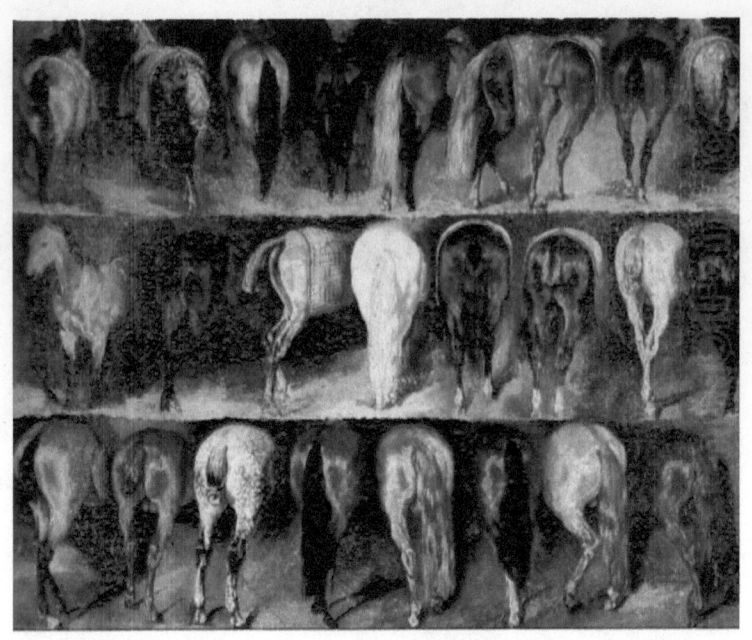

The Croups

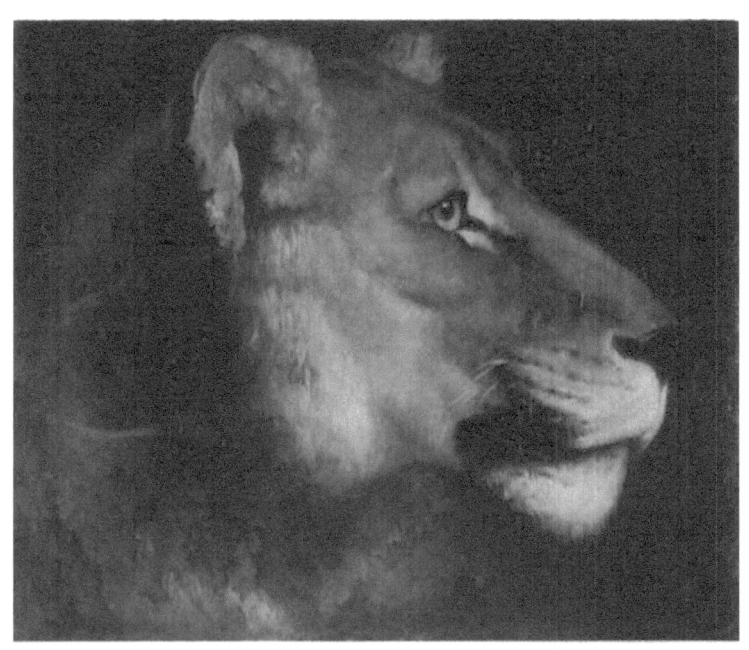

The head of lion

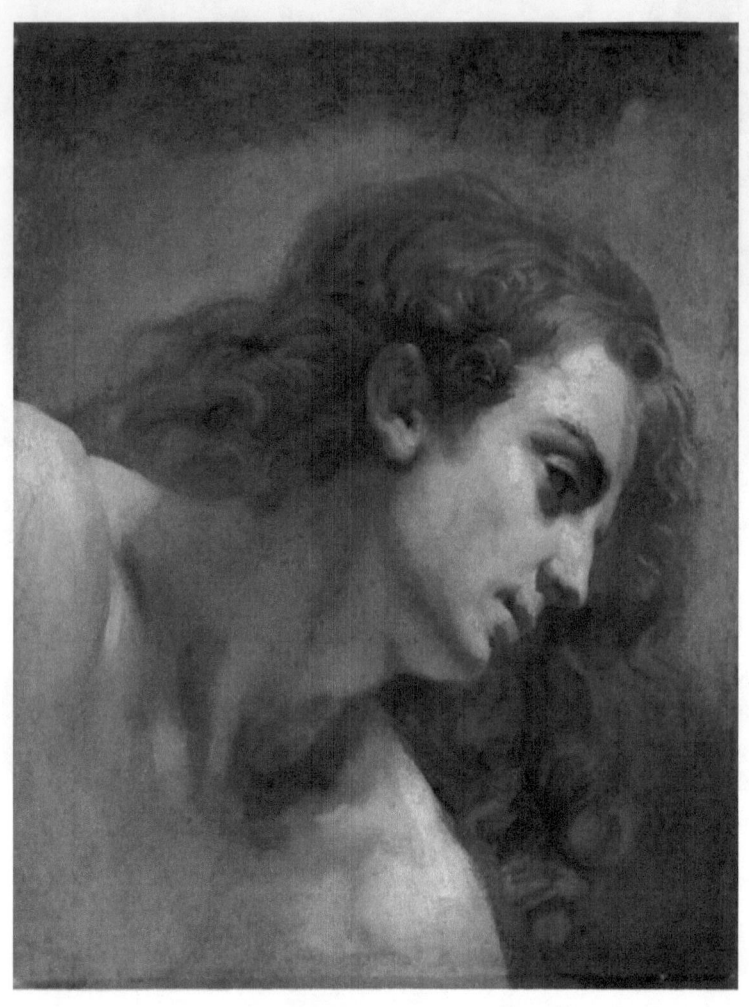

The head of young man
Oil on canvas

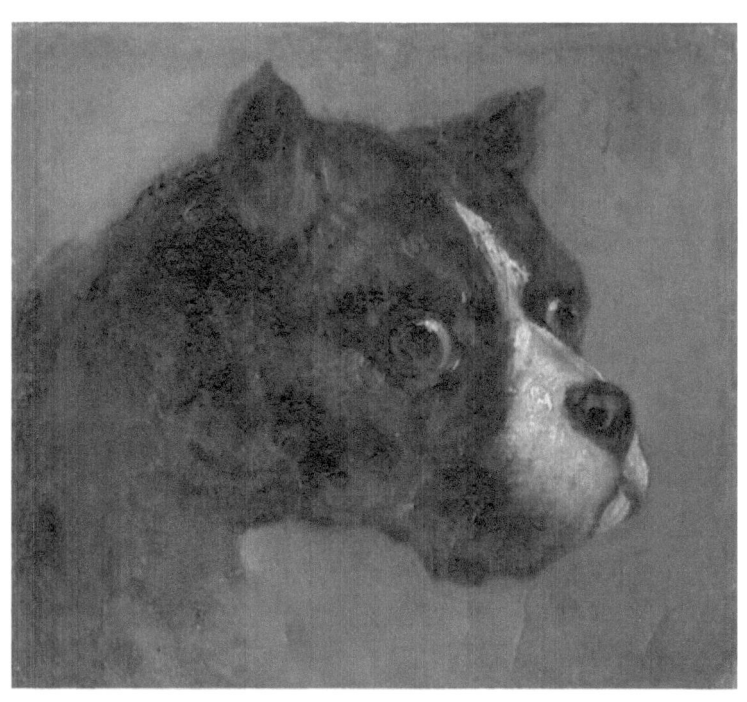

The head of bulldog
Oil on canvas

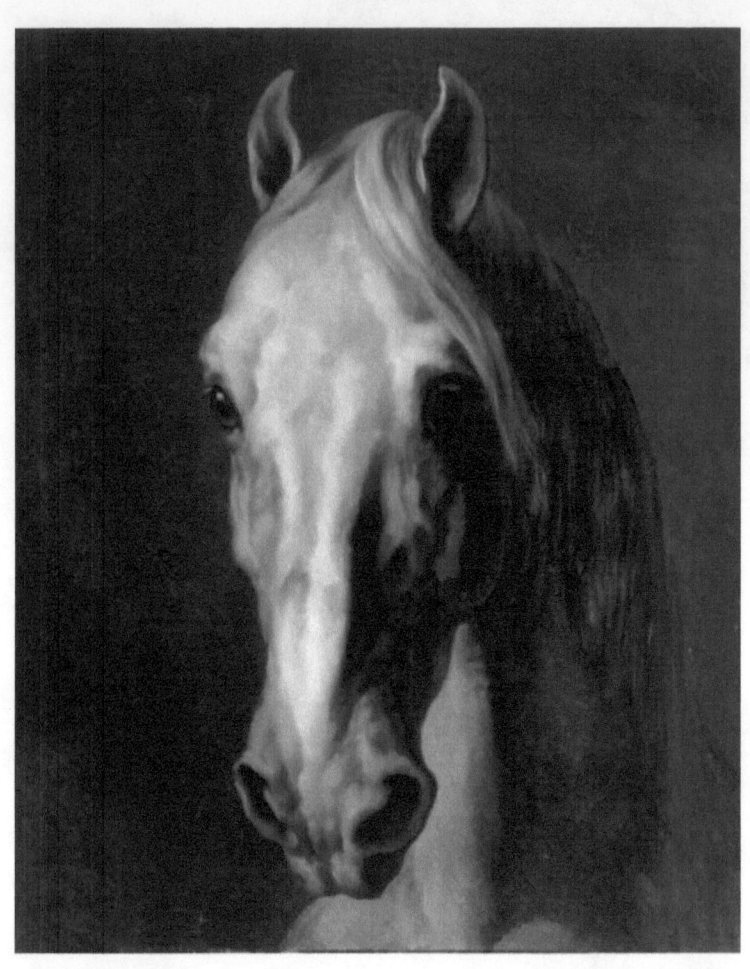

The head of white horse
Oil on canvas

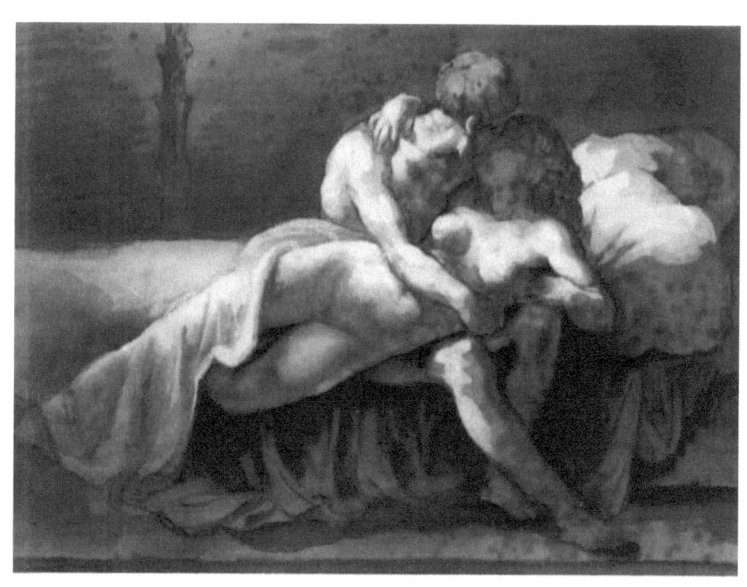

The Kiss

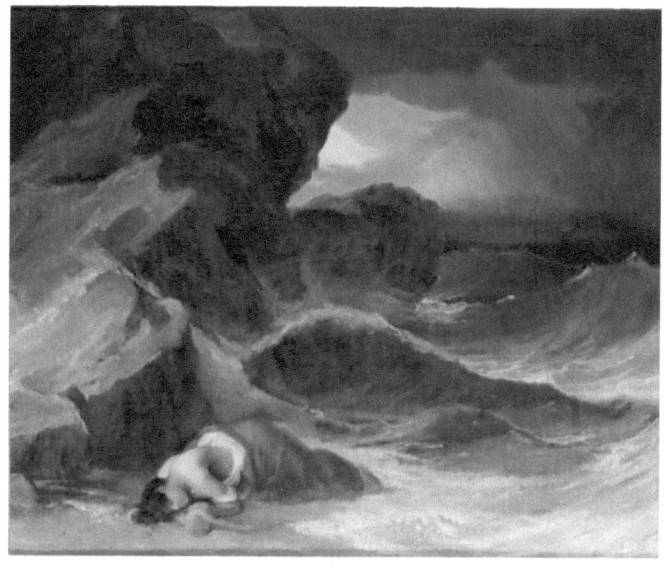

The Storm, or The Shipwreck, Oil on canvas

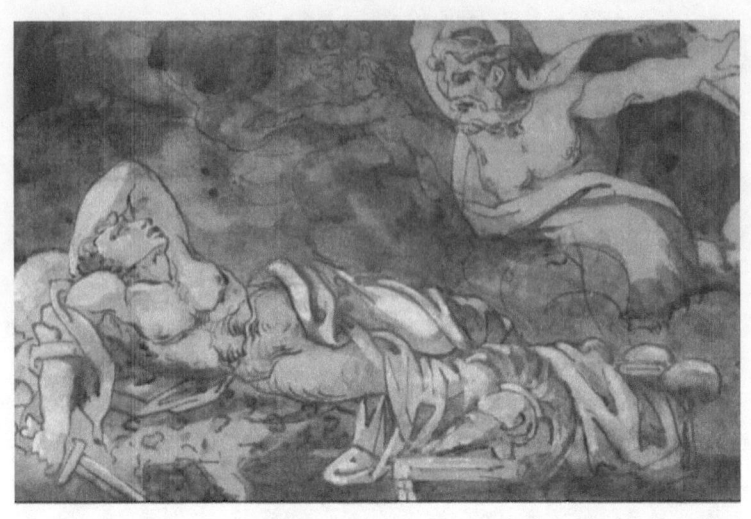

The Dream of Aeneas

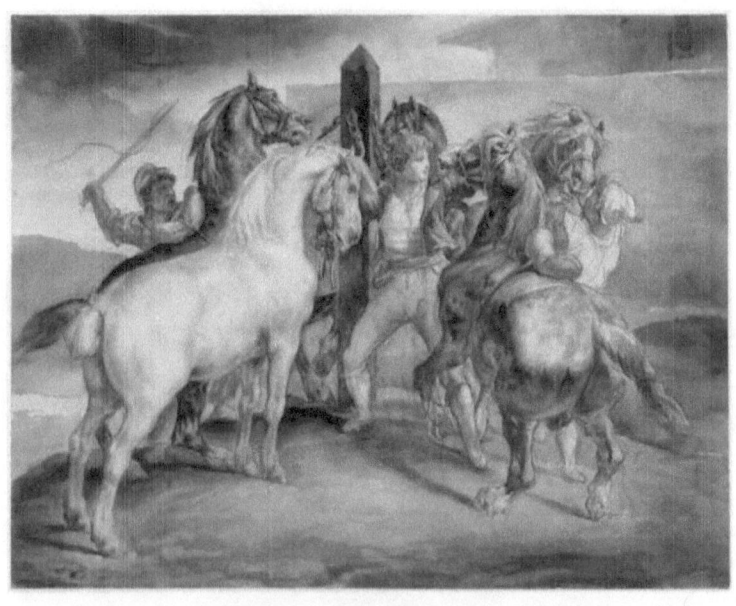

The Horse Market
Oil on canvas

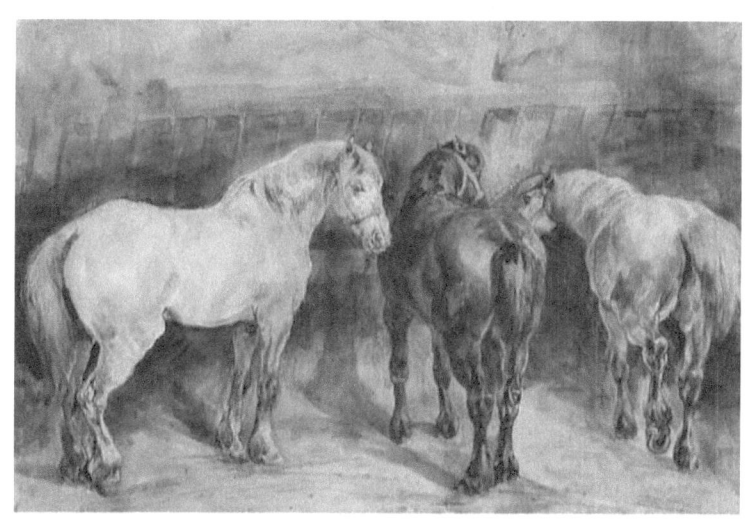

Three horses in their stable
Oil on canvas

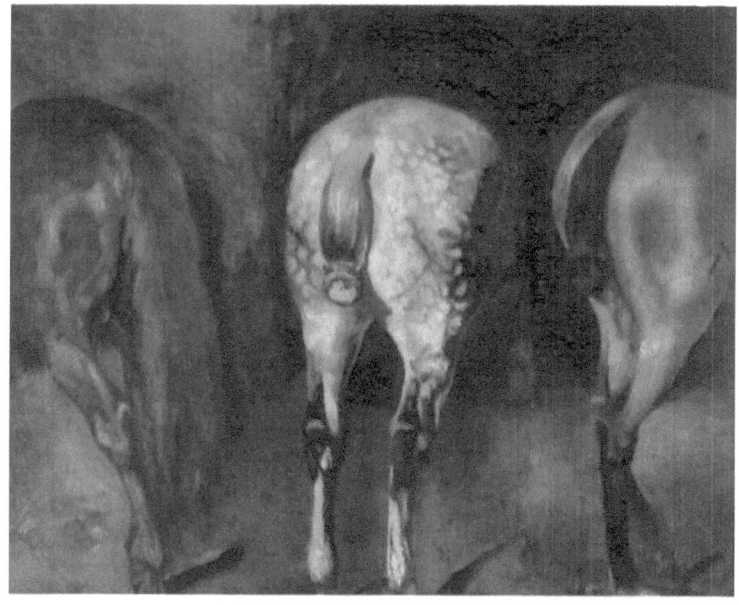

Three rumps of horses

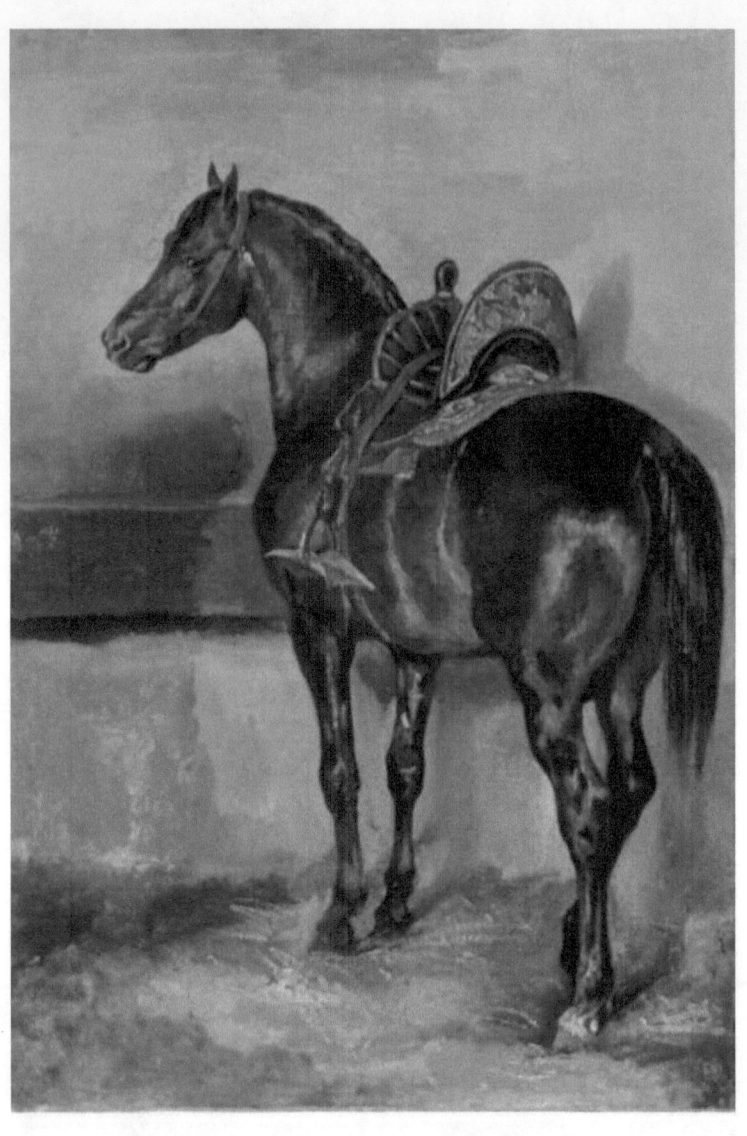

Turkish horse in a stable
Oil on canvas

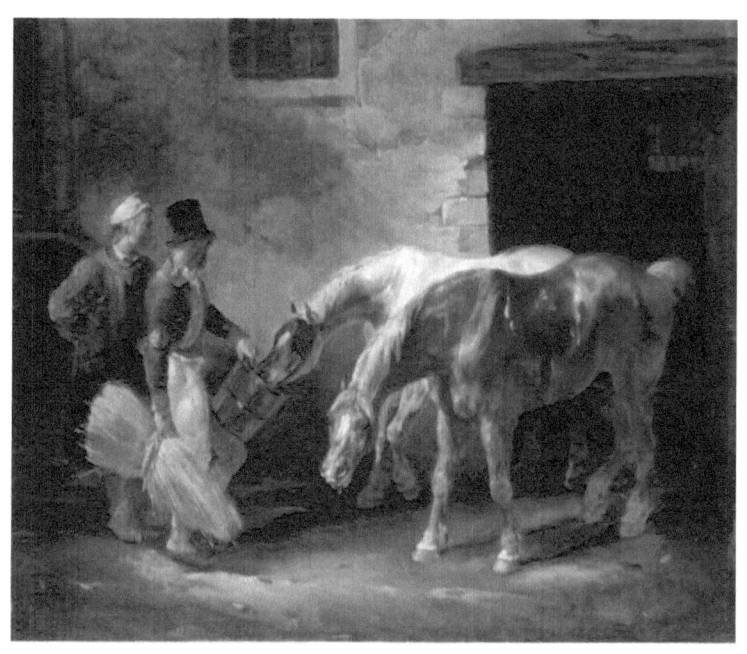

Two post-horses at the stable
Oil on canvas

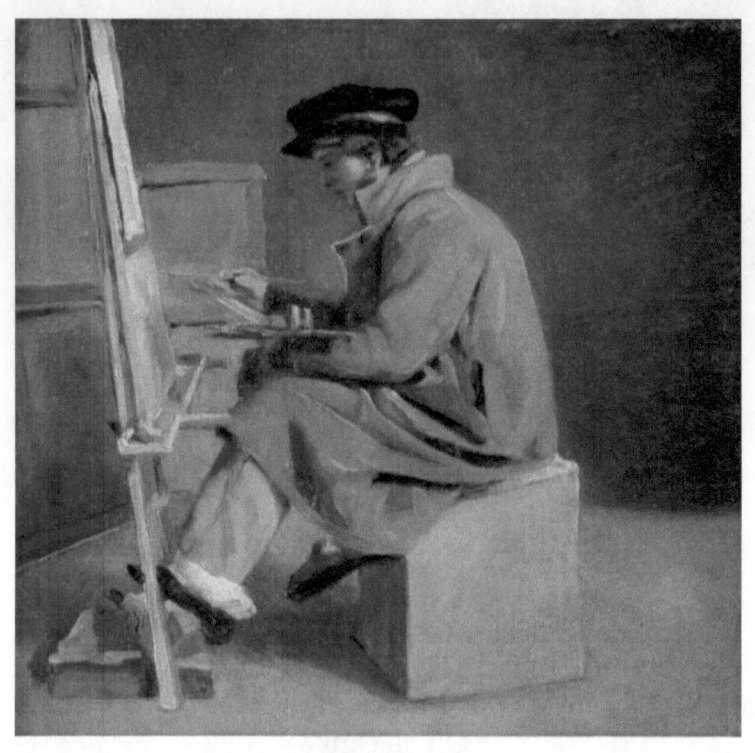

Young painter at his easel
Oil on canvas